THE PICTURE GALLERY
OF
CANADIAN HISTORY

The PICTURE GALLERY of CANADIAN HISTORY

Illustrations drawn & collected by
C.W.JEFFERYS, R.C.A., LL.D.
assisted by T.W.McLEAN

VOL. 2
1763 to 1830

The RYERSON PRESS-TORONTO

Tenth Printing, February, 1968

THE PICTURE GALLERY OF CANADIAN HISTORY

VOLUME   I: *Beginning to 1763*

VOLUME   II: *1763 to 1830*

VOLUME III: *1830 to 1890*

Over 600 pages of illustrations

1982

PRINTED AND BOUND IN CANADA
BY THE RYERSON PRESS, TORONTO

INTRODUCTION

FOR the period covered by this volume there are so many sources of information that it is difficult to make a selection limited to the space available.

Pictorial records especially are numerous. From the time of the siege of Quebec a succession of officers of the British army and navy stationed in Canada have left us drawings of the scenery, the settlements and the life of the new colony. Many of these were engraved and published as prints in England. Civilian authors and artists also visited the country and wrote and illustrated books which give much information concerning the period. Portrait painters from the old land and the United States toured the country or established themselves in the towns and depicted the likenesses of the men and women of the time.

Besides these pictorial documents, numerous buildings, public and domestic, still survive, though many of the earliest structures, being of wood, have disappeared through decay or from fire. Much furniture and a considerable number of other physical objects, dating from this period, such as costumes, weapons, vehicles, tools and vessels, are to be found in museums and in private houses.

In this period, too, the territory to be covered grows more extensive. The country was explored from coast to coast and to the Arctic, and the fur-trader, the missionary and the settler penetrated into hitherto unknown regions.

Over so wide a field it is manifestly impossible in a small volume to furnish anything like a complete reference book and the searcher must look for more detailed or specific information among the sources herein listed. I must reiterate that my purpose is merely to supply a guide to further research, and to indicate by a limited number of typical drawings the resources available. In particular with regard to portraits I have not attempted to give an adequate or well-rounded collection. Many omissions doubtless will be observed: some of these portraits are familiar and easily obtainable in other books on Canadian history. Some of those which I have included have been chosen not only because they illustrate personages in themselves more or less important, but also because they show details of costume, of official robes and military uniforms, styles of hairdressing, etc., as well as the physiognomical types of the period. For it is to be observed that the human face and its expression is affected by many factors; some intangible, such as occupation, the ideas and ideals of the time, social position; others more material, as food habits and certain fashion details. A comparison of these various human countenances will lead to a perception of the prevailing characteristic expression of the time. There are no grinning faces and no display of teeth, such as mark our present era of "look pleasant" photography. On the whole, our pioneer forefathers and mothers appear a rather grim lot, though on occasion the younger ladies may look sentimental or simpering, and the gentlemen arrogant or benevolently condescending.

It will be observed that many of the portraits are from drawings by myself. The originals from which these are taken are, in most cases, oil paintings, more or less darkened by time, or from somewhat dingy reproductions. Photographs of these originals do not generally make clear or satisfactory "half-tone" engravings. I have therefore translated them into pen or crayon drawings, but in so doing I have tried to make

vi

faithful copies of the original work, emphasizing the character and concentrating the interest on the features and on accessories such as hairdressing and costume, with as much clearness of detail as possible.

Similar considerations as have directed my selection of portraits have been followed in the choice of buildings, etc., included in this volume. Consequently I have omitted the pictures of some familiar houses easily accessible in other works, some which have been so remodelled or obscured by later additions that they show little of their earlier appearance, and others, interesting in themselves, which are not typical of the design or the methods of construction of the period. In addition to some buildings connected with important historical events and personages, I have tried to present specimens characteristic of various localities, and illustrative of the changing styles through the years of the country's development. Neither in the portraits nor the buildings, nor in other items, have I confined my selections rigidly to the date limits set forth in this volume: on occasion I have included later examples in order to show stages of development or to emphasize contrast; but in every such case I have tried to make this distinction clear.

The years covered by this volume were marked by two world events which profoundly affected social life in Canada as elsewhere: the Independence of the United States and the French Revolution. Two great migrations resulted from these upheavals: the coming of the Loyalists, and the influx of settlers in the eighteen-twenties and thirties. Though they differed essentially in character, each set its mark indelibly on the development of Canada.

Many of the Loyalists were Americans by birth or by a residence of some years on this continent. Those who went to the Maritime Provinces came for the most part from the sea-board districts of New England and the Middle and Southern colonies. They consisted largely of town dwellers and of inhabitants of long-settled rural areas, and consequently were Americans of some generations. The Upper Canada Loyalists came mainly from the interior sections of the middle colonies, New York, Pennsylvania, New Jersey, etc. Such settlers, therefore, were more familiar with frontier conditions and pioneer life.

These differences in the character of the two groups of Loyalists were reflected in their costumes. The Maritime refugees probably brought a larger proportion of cityfied and formal clothes. Thus we see by the portraits of early Nova Scotia judges that they wore full-bottomed wigs and ermine trimmed robes, while those of Upper Canada, such as Osgoode and Powell, depict them without these decorative accessions, and it is authoritatively stated that neither judges nor lawyers ever wore wigs in this province. We also learn from the letters of Mrs. Martin Hunter that the women of New Brunswick at an early date were uniformly given to finery. Other contemporary references seem to confirm this characteristic of the Maritime settlers. One gets no such impression of devotion to fashion among the Upper Canada settlers from Mrs. Simcoe's Diary, though at such functions as balls and assemblies at Newark and York ladies and gentlemen doubtless donned such fine raiment as they possessed, a little behind the mode though it may have been. In this connection may be noted the sensation which it is said the jewels of the French Royalist émigré, the Countess de Chalus, produced in York society. John Lambert remarks upon the slovenly, negligent and old-fashioned dress of the English inhabitants of Lower Canada. Scattered references in other sources mention buckskin, home-spun, and linsey-woolsey garments in use by both men and women among the Bay of Quinte Loyalists, kilts by the Highlanders, and remnants of military uniforms still being worn by soldiers of the Loyalist regiments long after their disbandment along the St. Lawrence and on the Niagara.

In contrast to these continental American settlers were the emigrants from England, Scotland and Ireland who flocked into the continent in the years of economic distress and political unrest which followed the cessation of the Napoleonic wars. Most of these new-comers were artisans, farm laborers, small tradesmen, discharged soldiers of the regular army, all of them entirely unacquainted with the conditions of life in the backwoods of America. Characteristic of this period and the following decade or more was the settlement of groups from special localities of the homeland by colonization promoters such as Colonel Talbot, Hon. Peter Robinson and the Canada Company, and by the Lanark, Rice Lake and other communities. Almost every district also contained some half-pay officers and gentry, and though all had to set themselves more or less to physical labor and generally do for themselves, the social distinctions of the old land persisted to a large extent and for many years. The former social status of the settler and his place of origin were shown by his clothing, his house and its furnishings, by his manners and customs. On his arrival, he (and she), wore such clothes as they were accustomed to in the old land, and these served them for some time in their new home. We find references to smock-frocks, to boots hob-nailed and ankle-high, to long corduroy trousers, gartered at the knee, and to women's shawls worn over head and shoulders, to pattens and clogs, home-made plaited straw hats and bonnets, to little girls' pinafores and pantalettes. Those who had been brought up in better circumstances brought with them some remnants of their former possessions, a few heirlooms, clothes of a finer cut and richer fabric, a party dress, some treasured chinaware, a few books, perhaps a family picture or two, and strove to give some adornment to the pioneer home.

Any pictorial reconstruction of this period of our past must take into account the contrasting character of these two migrations. The Loyalist settler and the post-Napoleon-war emigrant were markedly different, not only in their antecedents and their attitude of mind, but in their appearance. Attention must also be given to the social diversity pointed out by the foregoing references. A study of the numerous contemporary memoirs, letters and reminiscences is indispensable for an understanding of the conditions of the period. The most important of these are listed in the extensive bibliography included in this volume.

The illustrations, whether drawings of factual details or imaginative pictorial visualizations, are based on data gathered from these and similar sources of information, on objects in museums and private houses, and on authentic contemporary pictures.

In the third volume which will bring the pictorial story to the end of the nineteenth century, I shall not attempt to cover its enormous field, nor confine myself strictly to the period. I shall touch only upon some of its characteristic features and development, leaving many of its later topics to be sought in numerous easily accessible sources. In this concluding volume, also, I shall hope to find room for some subjects which, owing to lack of time and space, were omitted in the preceding books.

It is impossible to mention all who have helped me with information and advice over many years. I can make here only a general but most grateful acknowledgment of their encouragement and assistance.

CHARLES W. JEFFERYS.

York Mills,
Ontario.

x

CONTENTS

PART FOUR

PART ONE

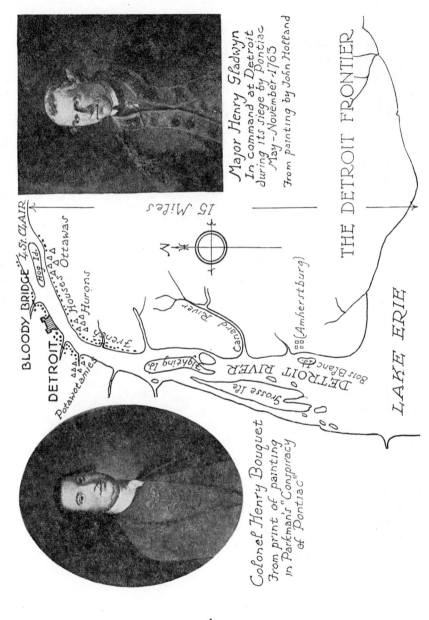

Major Henry Gladwyn
In command at Detroit
during its siege by Pontiac
May–November 1763
From painting by John Holland

THE DETROIT FRONTIER

LAKE ERIE

DETROIT RIVER

15 Miles

BLOODY BRIDGE "½ St. CLAIR

Hog Id.

Houses Ottawas

Hurons

French

Potawotamies

Detroit.

Grosse Ile

Fighting Id.

Bois Blanc Id.

Canard River

(Amherstburg)

Colonel Henry Bouquet
From print of painting
in Parkman's "Conspiracy
of Pontiac"

1

PONTIAC'S MEETING WITH GLADWYN AT DETROIT. 1763.

PRE-REVOLUTIONARY BUILDINGS *in* NOVA SCOTIA

C.W.JEFFERYS

House built
by *Sylvanus Cobb*
at *Liverpool.*

Roof of *Gambrel* or *Hip*
Type. Walls shingled.

Interior of
Meeting House

Meeting House built 1765 at
Barrington. Remodelled 1817.

INDIANS HUNTING BUFFALO

C. W. JEFFERYS

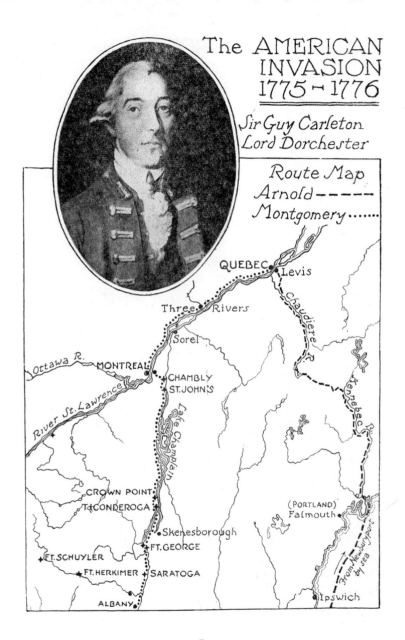

The AMERICAN
INVASION
1775 ~ 1776

Sir Guy Carleton
Lord Dorchester

Route Map
Arnold — — — —
Montgomery ....

QUEBEC ● Levis
Three ● Rivers
Chaudiere R.
● Sorel
Ottawa R.
MONTREAL ● CHAMBLY
ST.JOHN'S
River St.Lawrence
Lake Champlain
Kennebec R.
CROWN POINT
TICONDEROGA
Skenesborough
(PORTLAND)
Falmouth ●
FT.GEORGE
FT.SCHUYLER
FT.HERKIMER SARATOGA
From Newburyport by sea
ALBANY ●
Ipswich ●

5

AMERICAN REVOLUTIONISTS in CANADA

Benedict Arnold

Benjamin
Franklin
from portrait
by Duplessis
in
Philadelphia

Richard Montgomery

From portraits
in the Chateau
de Ramezay
Montreal

Mrs. Walker

Thomas Walker

DEATH OF MONTGOMERY

INDIAN LEADERS in the WAR of the REVOLUTION

Joseph Brant
From portrait in Indian Department, Washington

Colonel William Claus

Lt. Colonel John Butler

From portrait in Dominion Archives

Sir John Johnson

BURGOYNE & GERMAN MERCENARIES

Baron Friedrich A. Riedesel

Coat blue
Facings &
Vest yellow

Brunswick
Dragoon

Hessian
Grenadier
Coat blue
Facings
pink

Sir John Burgoyne

VIEWS IN OLD HALIFAX

Town Clock
Erected 1802
on Citadel Hill

Merchants sub-
scribed for the
building, & the
Military gave
the clock tower.

Gateway to
Dockyard
&
Clock
Tower of
1770

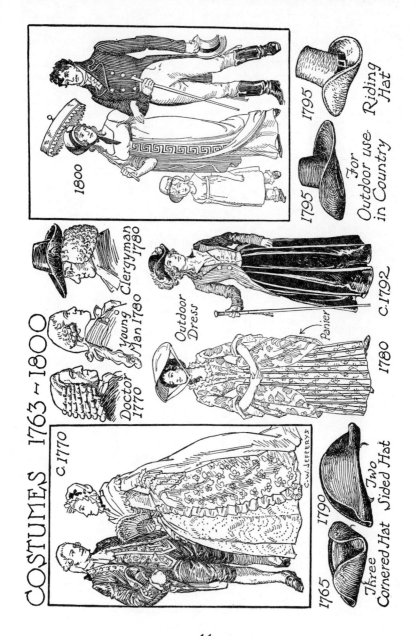

COSTUMES 1763~1800

1800

1795 Riding Hat

1795 For Outdoor use in Country

Clergyman 1780

Young Man 1780

Outdoor Dress

Doctor 1770

C.1792

Panier

1780

C.1770

C.W.JEFFERYS

1790 Two Sided Hat

1765 Three Cornered Hat

11

SAMUEL HEARNE ON HIS JOURNEY TO
THE COPPERMINE, 1770

12

MILITARY UNIFORMS 1775-1805

Green ← Black Velvet

← Red

Epaulette Buttons & Lace Silver — Quebec Artillery 1775 — Field Officer's Coat

Epaulette — Gilt Belt Plate — Coatee Lieutenant Quebec Militia — Skirt

Private, Regulars 1790

Private Regulars 1805

Captain 1805

13

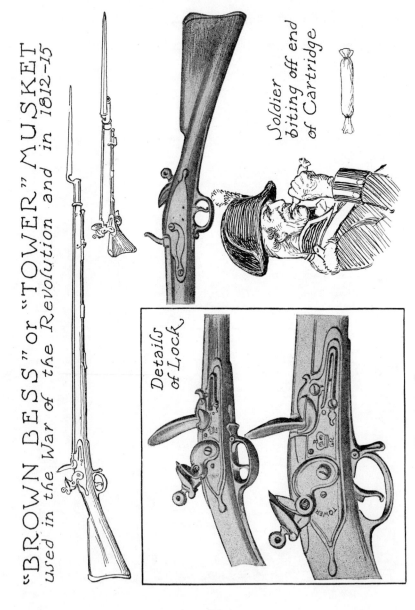

"BROWN BESS" or "TOWER" MUSKET
used in the War of the Revolution and in 1812-15

Soldier biting off end of Cartridge

Details of Lock

14

COOK and VANCOUVER

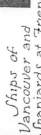

George Vancouver

From painting in National Portrait Gallery London.

Ships of Vancouver and Spaniards at Friendly Cove, Nootka, 1792.

James Cook

From portrait by Dance in Greenwich Hospital.

CAPTAIN COOK AT NOOTKA, 1778

C.W. JEFFERYS

Interior of Indian House at Nootka

*Village of Nootka.   Engraving
from drawing by John Webber, R.A.,
in Cook's "Voyage", 1784.*

17

WEST COAST NATIVES

From drawings by John Webber 1778

Nootka Indian, with Quiver, Bow & Arrows, & Hat of woven matting.

In Collection of David I. Bushnell Jr.

Interior of Nootka House

Nootka

Prince William Sound

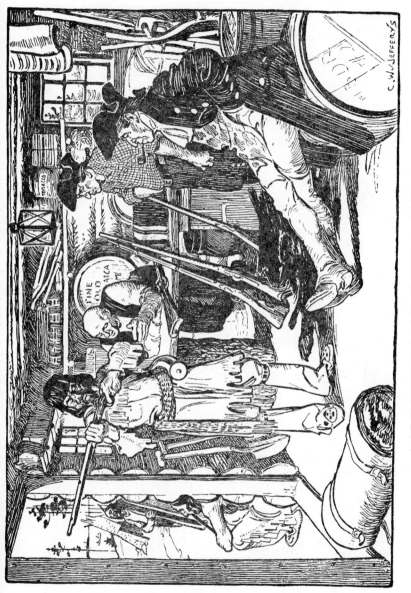

A FRONTIER TRADER'S STORE, ABOUT 1780

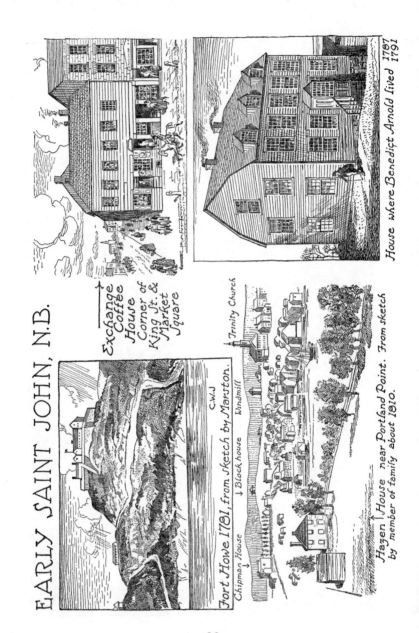

EARLY SAINT JOHN, N.B.

Exchange Coffee House Corner of King St. & Market Square

House where Benedict Arnold lived 1787 1791

Fort Howe 1781, from sketch by Marston. C.W.J

Chipman House Blockhouse Windmill Trinity Church

Hazen House near Portland Point. From sketch by member of family about 1810.

SHELBURNE THE LOYALIST CITY of REFUGE in NOVA SCOTIA

Leather Fire Bucket

Fire Engine given to Shelburne by King George III

Church built by the Loyalists

The Frith House built in 1783

ESTABLISHMENT of NEW BRUNSWICK GOVERNMENT

Legislative Building Fredericton, occupied 1788-1800.

1st Government House Fredericton

Mallard House, Saint John, where Assembly first met, Jan. 3, 1786.

Colonel Thomas Carleton, First Lieutenant Governor.

LOYALISTS ON THEIR WAY TO UPPER CANADA

C.W. JEFFERYS

LOYALISTS CAMPING ON THEIR WAY UP THE
ST. LAWRENCE, 1784

LOYALISTS DRAWING LOTS FOR THEIR LANDS, 1784

From drawing in possession of F. G. Venables, Esq.

JOSEPH BRANT AND MOHAWKS AT GRAND RIVER

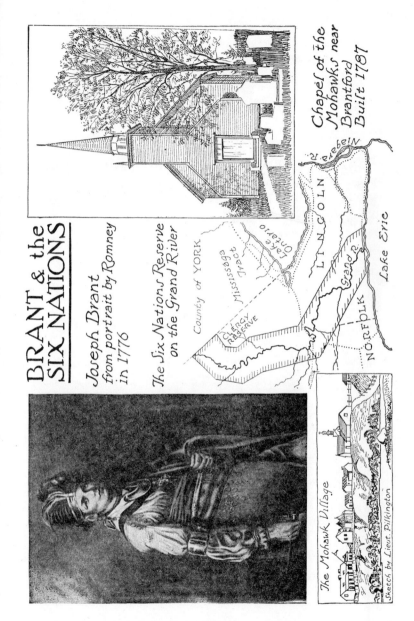

BRANT & the SIX NATIONS

Joseph Brant
from portrait by Romney in 1776

The Six Nations Reserve on the Grand River

Chapel of the Mohawks near Brantford Built 1787

County of YORK

Lake Ontario

Mississaga Tract

CLERGY RESERVE

L I N C O L N

Grand R.

Niagara R.

N O R F O L K

Lake Erie

The Mohawk Village

Sketch by Lieut. Pilkington

EARLY SURVEYORS

Major
Samuel Holland

Lieut-Colonel
Joseph Bouchette
From engraving
by J Thomson
after Englehart

Colonel
J F Wallet
des Barres

Holland House
on Ste Foye Road
Quebec
From Sketch in
Dominion Archives

Holland's
Astronomical
Clock

Portrait
owned by
Rev C W Vernon
Halifax

SAMUEL HEARNE & FORT PRINCE of WALES

Samuel Hearne
From his "Journey to the Northern Ocean", published 1795.

Aerial View of the Fort

Part of the Ruins with guns spiked & dismounted in 1782 ⟶

From Canadian Geographical Journal

Hearne's View of the Fort

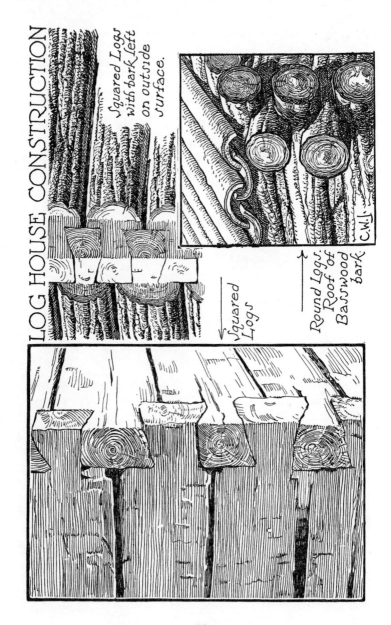

LOG HOUSE CONSTRUCTION

Squared Logs with bark left on outside surface.

Squared Logs

Round Logs. Roof of Basswood bark.

C.W.J.

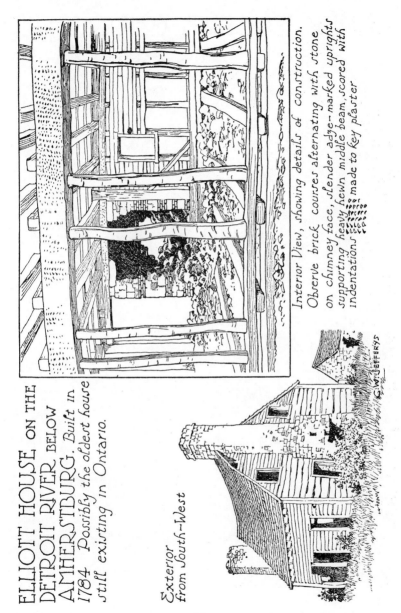

ELLIOTT HOUSE ON THE DETROIT RIVER BELOW AMHERSTBURG. Built in 1784 Possibly the oldest house still existing in Ontario.

Exterior from South-West

Interior View, showing details of construction.

Observe brick courses alternating with stone on chimney face, slender adze-marked uprights supporting heavy hewn middle beam, scored with indentations made to key plaster

C.W. JEFFERYS

31

EARLY ENGLISH CHURCHMEN
in CANADA

Rev.
John
Stuart
1st Rector of Kingston, U.C.

Rt. Rev.
Charles Inglis
First Bishop of Nova Scotia

Rev.
Jacob Mountain
1st Bishop of Quebec

Rev. John Ogilvie D.D.
after Copley. In Trinity Church, N.Y.

PROMINENT PERSONAGES of QUEBEC

"Samos", or "Woodfield House", residence of Adam Mabane. From drawing in the possession of P.B. Casgrain K.C., Quebec.

Dr Adam Mabane

Chief Justice William Smith

Peter Livius, Chief Justice

Herman. W. Ryland

33

Sir FREDERICK
HALDIMAND
and the
CHATEAU
QUEBEC

Rear of
Chateau
St. Louis

Chateau Haldimand
1784-1892

Chateau St. Louis, burnt 1834.

34

C.W.JEFFERYS

INDIAN TRADING FURS, 1785

35

C.W. JEFFERYS

PIONEER SOWING GRAIN IN HIS CLEARING

SURVEY · PARTY · 1793.

From drawing by D. F. Thomson, in Toronto Art League Calendar, 1897.

The FIRST SHIP BUILT on the PACIFIC
Launching of the "North-West America"
at Nootka Sound, September 19, 1788.
"From Meares's Voyages"

Captain
John Meares

ALEXANDER MACKENZIE
and his EXPLORATIONS

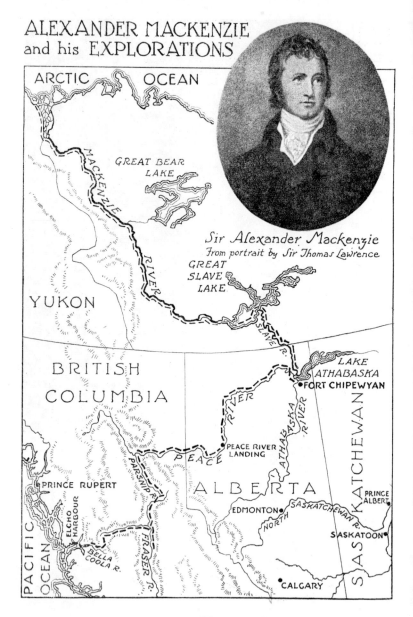

ARCTIC OCEAN

GREAT BEAR LAKE

MACKENZIE RIVER

YUKON

Sir Alexander Mackenzie
From portrait by Sir Thomas Lawrence

GREAT SLAVE LAKE

BRITISH COLUMBIA

SLAVE R.

PEACE RIVER

LAKE ATHABASKA

• FORT CHIPEWYAN

ATHABASKA RIVER

PEACE RIVER LANDING

ALBERTA

SASKATCHEWAN

• PRINCE RUPERT

PARSNIP R.

FRASER R.

ELCHO HARBOUR

BELLA COOLA R.

PACIFIC OCEAN

EDMONTON •

NORTH SASKATCHEWAN R.

PRINCE ALBERT

SASKATOON •

• CALGARY

40

MACKENZIE AT THE ARCTIC, 1789

C.W. JEFFERYS

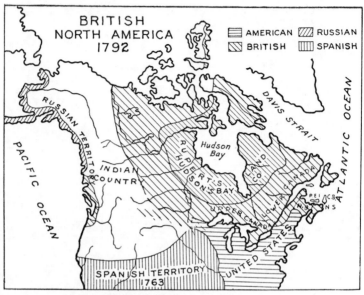

BRITISH
NORTH AMERICA
1792

AMERICAN   RUSSIAN
BRITISH   SPANISH

DAVIS STRAIT

ATLANTIC OCEAN

RUSSIAN TERRITORY

PACIFIC OCEAN

INDIAN COUNTRY

Hudson Bay

RUPERT'S HUDSON'S BAY

LAND CO.

LOWER CANADA

P.E.I. C.B.I.
N.S.

UPPER CANADA

UNITED STATES

SPANISH TERRITORY
1763

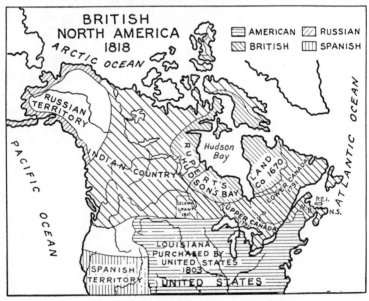

BRITISH
NORTH AMERICA
1818

AMERICAN   RUSSIAN
BRITISH   SPANISH

ARCTIC OCEAN

ATLANTIC OCEAN

RUSSIAN TERRITORY

PACIFIC OCEAN

INDIAN COUNTRY

Hudson Bay

RUPERT'S HUDSON'S BAY

LAND CO. 1670

LOWER CANADA 1791

P.E.I.
C.B.
N.S.

UPPER CANADA 1791

SELKIRK GRANT 1811

LOUISIANA
PURCHASED BY
UNITED STATES
1803

SPANISH
TERRITORY

UNITED STATES

42

EARLY KINGSTON

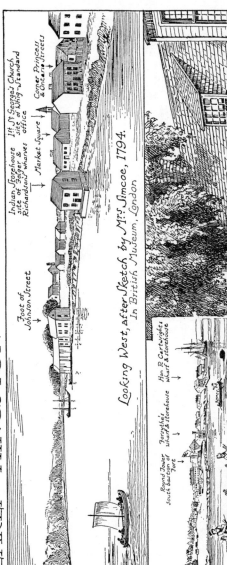

Foot of Johnston Street

Indian Storehouse site or 3¢ 9¢ & Richardson wharves

Market Square

1st St George's Church site of Whig-Standard office

Corner Princess & Ontario Streets

Looking West, after Sketch by Mrs Simcoe, 1794.
In British Museum, London

Round Tower South bastion of Fort

Forsythe's wharf & storehouse

Hon. R Cartwright's wharf & storehouse

From Drawing by Ensign James Peachey
showing eastern end of Cataraqui 1783

House formerly on Queen Street, next to Saint Paul's Church in which Lieutenant-Governor Simcoe is said to have first met his Executive Council in 1792. It has been removed & now stands in Kiwanis Square, on Rideau Street.

43

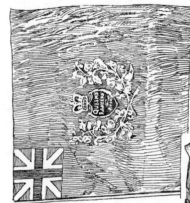

Presented to the City of Toronto by Col. F. B. Robins.

The QUEEN'S RANGERS

1777 Colours of the Rangers, now in the Public Library, Toronto.

A Rifleman of the Rangers

C. W. JEFFERYS

THE FIRST CAPITAL OF UPPER CANADA

NEWARK, NOW NIAGARA-ON-THE-LAKE

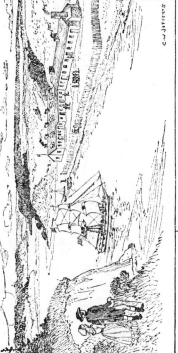

C.W.JEFFERYS

Only Surviving building of Navy Hall.

Newark & the Mouth of the Niagara River in 1792,

showing Navy Hall & H.M.S. Onondaga
From sketch by Mrs. Simcoe.

The group of buildings called Navy Hall,
on the river bank below Fort George, was
built by Gov. Haldimand to house stores
for the Provincial Navy. Simcoe added
a Council Chamber, in which the 1st
Legislative Assembly met, as appears
from Lieut-Governor's proclamation,
August, 1794. Most of the buildings
were burned by the Americans in 1813.

C.W.JEFFERYS & T.W.MℓL.

45

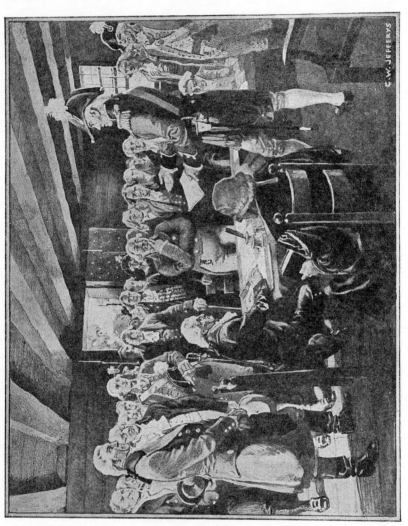

LIEUTENANT-GOVERNOR SIMCOE OPENING THE FIRST
LEGISLATIVE ASSEMBLY OF UPPER CANADA, 1792

MEETING OF THE FIRST LEGISLATIVE ASSEMBLY
OF LOWER CANADA, 1792

47

SIMCOE LANDING AT TORONTO 1793

The view of the Harbour is from a sketch by Mrs Simcoe

White
Black
White
Red
White
Green
White
Black

Private
5th Northumberland
Fusiliers. 1792

C.W. JEFFERYS

48

Francis Simcoe
from a sketch by
Lieut. Pilkington. 1796

Mrs. Simcoe,
in Welsh dress.

From
The Diary of Mrs. Simcoe"
by J. Ross Robertson.

Lieutenant-Governor
John Graves Simcoe.
From the memorial by
Flaxman, in Exeter
Cathedral

Castle Frank,
the Simcoes' country
house on the Don
from
Sketch by Mrs. Simcoe

THE SIMCOES AND CASTLE FRANK

49

SIMCOE AT THE BUILDING OF FORT YORK, 1793

NOTES ON PART ONE

Page 3

Barrington was founded by settlers from Cape Cod and Nantucket in 1761, many of them descendants of the *Mayflower* Pilgrims. The Meeting House, built 1765, was used for many years by all denominations. See *Down in Nova Scotia*, by Clara Dennis, Chap. XV.

Liverpool was settled by New Englanders in 1759. Among them was Capt. Sylvanus Cobb, who had served as a Ranger at the first siege of Louisbourg in 1745. For ten years he commanded an armed sloop, and conveyed many settlers to Nova Scotia. He acted as pilot of Wolfe's vessel at the second siege of Louisbourg in 1758. At the siege of Havana in 1762 he was attacked by yellow fever, to which he succumbed, lamenting that he could not have died in battle. His house, built 1759, has a gambrel roof and shingle-covered walls; a type common to the Atlantic Coast from Nantucket to New Brunswick. See *More About Nova Scotia*, by Clara Dennis, Chap. XX.

Page 6

Thomas Walker, a merchant and magistrate of Montreal, and his wife were active sympathizers with the American invaders. Walker, in Governor Murray's time, had made himself obnoxious to the authorities over the billetting of officers of the British army in private houses. He was the victim of an assault made by several soldiers, who were never identified, who invaded his house at night. In the struggle he was severely beaten, and a piece of one of his ears cut off. On the return in May, 1776, of the American delegates, Carrol, Chase and Franklin, to the United States from their unsuccessful mission to Canada, the Walkers thought it wise to leave Montreal with them. Franklin, in a letter concerning their journey, says of them: "The Walkers took such liberties in taunting at our conduct in Canada that it almost came to a quarrel. We continued our care of her, however, and landed her safely in Albany with her three wagon-loads of baggage, brought hitherto without putting her to any expense, and parted civilly, though coldly. I think they both have an excellent talent in making themselves enemies, and I believe they will never be long without them."

Page 7

On the morning after the attack by Montgomery at the Près-de-ville barricade, a blood-stained fur cap, marked in the lining R.M., was found in the snow outside the barrier. All the bodies were brought into the city, and that of Montgomery was identified by his A.D.C. and other Americans who had been captured. This information is given in *Lindsay's Journal of the Siege of Quebec*.

Montgomery was buried with military honors on the night of January 4th near St. Louis Gate, the service being read by the garrison chaplain. In 1818 the body was exhumed, and taken to the city of New York, where it was re-buried under a monument in front of St. Paul's Church on Broadway.

Page 9

In 1776 the British Government hired from the Duke of Brunswick-Lunebourg 4,000 German soldiers for service in Canada. They were under the command of Major-General Baron Friedrich Adolphus von Riedesel, born in Hesse, 1738. He had served in Europe during the Seven Years' War. He took part with his mercenary troops in Burgoyne's campaign of 1777, and was made prisoner at the surrender of Saratoga. He was exchanged in 1780 and returned to Canada, where he remained until his departure to Europe. He held various commands until his death at Brunswick in 1800. Over 1,200 of these German soldiers remained in Canada, and became incorporated with the French-Canadian population.

His wife, Frederika von Masson, a spirited and intrepid woman, with her young daughters accompanied Riedesel throughout the campaign. See *Un Général Allemand au Canada*, by Georges Monarque, and Bruce Lancaster's novel, *Guns of Burgoyne*, which gives a vivid and accurate picture of the personages and events of the period.

Page 11

During the early part of this period women's smart dresses were fashioned with *paniers*, worn over the sides of the skirt, which was supported by a hoop. These both disappeared by about 1790 when fashion changed to a high-waisted, loose, one-piece garment, which was supposed to imitate classical drapery. Every woman tried to look like a Greek or Roman statue. About

52

this time, too, came in the use of shawls woven with Oriental designs, known later as Paisley shawls. In harmony with these dresses were the furniture and room decoration of the time, the Empire style. The illustrations show the dress of fashionable society; but it must be remembered that among the pioneers clothing was of heavier and stouter materials, suited to their occupations and surroundings, and that the few fine dresses which they possessed were of an older fashion.

Three of the numerous styles of men's wigs are shown. By the end of the century they were rapidly disappearing, and men were wearing their own hair, though generally dressed in much the same way as the wigs. With the coming of the classical style they began to cut it shorter at the back and dress it higher on the head.

The evolution of men's hats is seen in the gradual change from the three-cornered eighteenth century hat to the riding hat, the forerunner of the stiff, high, "top" hat of the next century

Page 13

Epaulettes were introduced into the British army by Royal Warrant of 19th Dec., 1768. This prescribed that cavalry officers should have an "embroidered or laced Epaulette of Gold or Silver, with Fringe, on the *Left* Shoulder," with the exception of Light Dragoons, who were to have one on *each* shoulder; while infantry officers should wear a similar epaulette "on the *Right* Shoulder," with the exception of officers of the Grenadier Company of each Regiment, who were to have one on *each* shoulder.

From information kindly supplied by the late Col. Jabez Elliott, M.D.

These regulations seem to have applied to officers up to the rank of Captain, while superior or "field" officers generally wore two epaulettes.

The crescent of bronze or silver worn at the throat of officers was the gorget, a reduced survival of the piece of earlier armor which protected the neck. They were also given to Indian war chiefs: Romney's portrait of Brant shows him wearing one. This custom was followed for some time after the gorget was abolished in the British army. Doubtless its use persisted among the Indians with whom it was popular both as an ornament and as an insignia of the wearer's rank.

53

Page 14

The early cartridge was made of a charge of powder and a bullet wrapped in paper, and tied at the ends. The soldier bit off one end and poured the contents into the muzzle of the musket, which was held upright while being loaded and the charge pounded down with the ramrod seen in the drawing in a slot on the under side of the barrel. The soldier was clean shaven, but in battle his lips became blackened with powder from biting the cartridges. It is said that skulls unearthed at Lundy's Lane eighty years after the battle showed front teeth blackened by cartridge powder. The bayonet blade was three sided, and set to one side of a hollow stock which fitted over the musket muzzle.

Page 16

In the narrative of Captain Cook's last voyage will be found detailed descriptions of the West Coast Indians, their houses, clothing, tools, etc., as they were in 1778. Also included are several engravings from drawings made by John Webber, R.A., the official artist attached to the expedition.

Cook says that the houses of the Nootka Indians were about seven or eight feet high, the back part higher than the front, made of hewn planks, with the sloping roof boards laid loosely so as to be removable for light, air and the escape of smoke. At the end farthest from the door were placed large tree trunks, carved into shapes of men, beasts and birds, and painted in vivid colours. None of Webber's drawings show these so-called totem poles *outside* the houses. The only tools for wood working possessed by the natives before the white men came were implements of bone and stone for carving, and coarse-scaled fish skins for polishing. Cook found that some of them had pieces of iron, brass and copper, which were fixed to handles to form chisels or gouges. These metals had been procured in trade from Indians in contact with the whites, or from Spanish and Russian ships. With the possession of steel tools obtained from the trading vessels which frequented the coast after Cook's explorations, the native art of carving rapidly developed to a high degree of finish. Totem poles became taller and more elaborately carved, and were now placed outside the houses. These exterior poles therefore date only from the time of the white men's arrival, and most of those now surviving are probably much later. Several specimens are to be seen in Canadian museums.

Mention is also made of frames of thin poles on which were hung fish to dry in the sun outside the houses, as shown in the drawing, which is based on Webber's picture of the Nootka village.

Cook describes the clothing of the Coast Indians as being made of pine bark fibres plaited together and of wool which "seems to be taken from different animals." Over these garments was frequently thrown the skin of a bear, wolf, or sea otter. Sometimes they wore carved wooden masks or visors, applied on the face, or to the upper part of the head. Some resembled human faces, others the heads of birds and of sea and land animals. Hats made of fine matting were also worn.

He remarks on the eagerness of the natives to obtain metal, stealing it in addition to getting all they could by trading. Brass, in particular, was sought after so keenly that hardly a bit of it was left in the ships except what belonged to their necessary instruments. Whole suits of clothing were stripped of every button, and copper kettles, candlesticks and canisters all went to wreck. In exchange the natives gave the valuable skins of the sea otter. In the drawing one of the Indians is shown trying to induce a sailor to part with his sleeve buttons.

Page 17

John Webber (1752-1793) was born in London of Swiss parentage. He was appointed draftsman on Cook's last voyage in 1776. He made many drawings of the scenery and inhabitants of the South Sea islands, and of the northern coasts of America and Asia. He was present at Cook's death, of which he later made a drawing. On his return to England he was engaged for some years in preparing the drawings and supervising the engravings made from them, which were published in the official narrative of the expedition. He was elected a member of the Royal Academy, and gained a considerable reputation as a landscape painter.

Observe in the interior view the fish hung from the rafters to dry in the smoke.

Page 20

James Simonds was a partner in a trading company formed in 1764 to carry on business at the River St. John. He is regarded as the founder of the first permanent settlement at the mouth of the river. Born at Haverhill, Massachusetts, and died in the house he had built at Portland Point, Saint John, at the age of ninety years. Several of his descendants were prominent in the community. The portrait on p. 220 shows him late in life.

William Hazen, also born in Haverhill, was a member of the same firm and related to Simonds. Settled at Saint John and in 1773 built a house at Portland Point (shown in the illustration), which was the best and most substantial until then erected. He was the ancestor of a family distinguished in the history of the province. *The River St. John*, by Rev. W. O. Raymond, gives much valuable information on the early days of the locality.

Fort Howe was built by Major Studholme on the high ground north of the harbour.

Benjamin Marston, a merchant at Marblehead, Mass., and an active Loyalist, was employed in 1784 as chief surveyor in laying out the town of Shelburne, N.S., in 1783. Next year he went to New Brunswick as Deputy Surveyor of the King's Woods, in supervision of timber for the Royal Navy. There are many references to him in *Winslow Papers*, by Rev. W. O. Raymond.

Page 21

Shelburne, previously known as Port Roseway, the most extensive settlement of the Loyalists in Nova Scotia, was established on a fine harbour on the south-west coast of the province. Governor Parr at the request of a number of New England refugees granted them a large tract of land, sent surveyors to lay out the lots and the streets of the projected town, and provided the settlers with lumber for their houses, and provisions for their first year. With unintentional irony he named the new city of refuge after the British minister whose administration had accepted the terms of the Treaty of Versailles, which had left the Loyalists at the mercy of the victorious Revolutionists, and which was largely responsible for their present plight. In May, 1783, about 4,000 settlers arrived, and within a couple of years the new town contained about 10,000 inhabitants. Shipyards, wharves, churches, shops, taverns and sawmills were quickly erected, fish and lumber were exported to the West Indies and Great Britain, a South American whaling industry was established, newspapers were published. Shelburne became the centre of a fashionable society, and it was predicted that it would supersede Halifax as the capital. But its period of prosperity was short: the neighbourhood was not capable of supporting the numbers who had so suddenly flocked into it, and many of the settlers were ill-suited to pioneer life. Within a few years most of its inhabitants had given up the unsuccessful struggle and departed, many of the houses were taken down and removed to Saint John and Halifax, others were burned or fell into decay. Instead of a busy metropolis, Shelburne today is a quiet, secluded and picturesque town, where a few fine old houses remain to mark its brief splendour and its shattered hopes.

In the early days of settlement, numerous regulations were established in Canada to protect the villages and towns against the danger of fire that constantly threatened and often destroyed the wooden houses. Thus in 1777 the law directed that chimneys were to be swept frequently to prevent the accumulation of soot, and ladders were to be attached to the roof so that the chimney could be reached if it caught fire; each house had to be provided with two poles ten feet long, with hooks, or with cross-bars at six-inch intervals, to be used for knocking off the roofs when in danger or on fire, with hatchets, and with two buckets, of leather, or wood iron hooped, which were to be kept constantly filled with water and placed inside conveniently near the door. Town houses situated close together had to be built with their gable ends of stone raised three feet above the roof to act as a barrier to the spread of fire. The fire engine at Shelburne was one of the earliest types of the hand-pumping machine which later of larger size and operated by more men remained in use until well into the nineteenth century when the steam-pumping engine displaced it.

Page 22

Thomas Carleton, born in Ireland, 1735, entered the army, and after some years of active service was sent to Canada in 1776 as Quarter Master General under his brother, Sir Guy Carleton, Governor and Commander-in-Chief. In 1784 he was appointed Lieutenant-Governor of the new province of New Brunswick. Established the capital at Fredericton, returned to England in 1803, where he died in 1817.

Page 27

At the close of the Revolutionary War the territory of the Six Nation Indians passed by treaty into the possession of the United States. To compensate those of them who had supported the British cause lands were given them in Upper Canada. A number of the Mohawks settled near Deseronto on the Bay of Quinte; but most of that tribe removed to a tract of land extending for six miles on either side along the Grand River which was granted to them by Governor Haldimand in 1784. With them came the Cayugas and members of other tribes of the Iroquois League. Their descendants still occupy these localities, though the greater portion of the Grand River territory has been purchased from them long since for white settlement.

The Society for the Propagation of the Gospel in Foreign Parts early in the eighteenth century had established a mission to the Mohawks. After their settlement in Upper Canada it continued its interest in them by the support of missionaries, the publication of Brant's translations of the Gospel of St. Mark, and the Church of England Prayer Book, etc., and by the maintenance of schools for Indian children. The old Mohawk church possesses a folio Bible and some of the silver communion vessels which Queen Anne in 1712 presented to "Her Majesty's Chapel of the Mohawks," the others being preserved by the church on the Deseronto Reserve. In the graveyard of the Grand River chapel are the tombs of Joseph Brant and his son John, and other chiefs of the tribe. It will be observed that in Lieut. Pilkington's sketch the spire of the church is different from that of today. The map is taken from the William Chewett Map of Upper Canada, dated 1813. See *Grand River*, by Mabel Dunham.

Page 28

Samuel Holland (1713-1801) at an early age joined the British army as lieutenant of engineers and served in Europe. Promoted captain in 1756, and appointed aide-de-camp to Wolfe. Served at Louisbourg, and while there gave instruction in surveying to Captain Simcoe of the navy, father of the first lieutenant-governor of Upper Canada. Under Captain Simcoe, James Cook while serving as master in his ship at the siege of Quebec and later the celebrated circumnavigator, learned the rudiments of marine surveying. Holland was engineer in chief at the siege of Quebec.

In 1763 he was appointed Surveyor-General of Quebec and Director of Surveys in British North America. Many of his maps are in the Archives at Ottawa. Holland House was Montgomery's headquarters during the siege of Quebec in 1775.

Joseph Frederic Wallet des Barres, born in England in 1722, of French Huguenot ancestry, died at Halifax, N.S., in 1824, at the age of 102. Served as lieutenant in the 60th Regiment in America. Rose to the rank of Brevet Colonel, Lieut.-Governor of Cape Breton, 1784-1787, and of Prince Edward Island, 1805-1812. Founded Sydney, N.S., 1785. Des Barres surveyed the coasts of the Maritime Provinces, and made many fine maps and views, which were published in his great work, *The Atlantic Neptune.* A magnificent set of these volumes is in the Archives of Canada.

Joseph Bouchette, born at Quebec 1774, died 1841, was the son of Jean Bouchette. The father had been in the government service under the French régime and after the British conquest entered the Provincial Navy, in which he attained the rank of Commodore. He conducted the escape of Governor Sir Guy Carleton from Montreal on the approach of Montgomery's army in 1775, conveying him and his aides, disguised as habitants, in an open boat past the American vessels and land batteries commanding the river. Joseph, the son, served in the Provincial Navy under his father until 1796-1797. He made the first survey of Toronto harbour in 1793. In 1804 he was appointed Surveyor-General of Lower Canada. In 1815, aided by a money grant from the legislature, he published his *Topographical Description of Lower Canada* in 1815, and on promise of the purchase of a number of copies of a new work went to England in 1829 to supervise the production of his *British Dominions in North America*, which was published in three volumes in London in 1832. These works contain many fine maps and engravings of Canadian scenery. Bouchette presented a de-luxe copy to King William IV at a special audience, and a collection of engravings from his sketches to the Duchess of Kent, on which occasion he saw the Princess Victoria, her daughter, the future Queen, then at the age of fourteen. The legislature failed to purchase the promised copies, and Bouchette's undertaking resulted in a serious financial loss to him.

Observe various styles of hair-dressing at different dates.

Fort Prince of Wales is situated at the mouth of Churchill River, on Hudson Bay. Its construction began in 1733 and was completed in 1771. It was captured and destroyed by a French naval force under La Pérouse in 1782. It has been partially restored and many of its guns remounted, and is now under the supervision of the National Parks Bureau.

This house, on Lot 5, Malden Township, on the Detroit River, is one of the few surviving buildings of the earliest period of Upper Canada settlement. The house is marked on a map of 1796 as one of six on the river front below Amherstburg. The United States Commissioners to the Western Indians were the guests of Captain Elliott, and the Journal of General Benjamin Lincoln, one of the Commissioners, has this reference, under date of July 21, 1793: "Captain Elliott received us with hospitality, and gave us the use of his house, garden, etc. . . . We had a full supply of boiled green corn, which was well grown. . . . Elliott has the best farm in the country I have seen, by far." In October of the next year Lieutenant-Governor Simcoe spent some days at Elliott's, on his expedition to the Miami. It is probable also that here took place the famous meeting between Brock and Tecumseh in 1812.

Matthew Elliott (1739-1814) was a trader with the Indians, who later became Deputy Superintendent in the Indian Department. He settled on the Detroit River after the American Revolution. He was Colonel of the 1st Essex Militia (1798-1814) and member of the House of Assembly for that county, 1800-1812. He served at the capture of Detroit, at Fort Meigs, Moravian Town, and Black Rock.

The present half-ruinous condition of the house enables us to see the method of its construction, which probably was that of many of the better houses of the time. It is a frame of hewn beams resting on a double wooden sill. It was sheathed and plastered inside, and covered by clapboards outside, with the exception of the south side of the lower storey, which is built of squared logs butting on the uprights of the frame. Between the upper and lower storeys are placed two sets of joists, the lower ones running lengthwise of the house, the upper ones resting on them crosswise and parallel with the gables, with their ends protruding outside under the eaves. The chimneys extend beyond the frame, that on the north being entirely outside the wall and placed nearer the western front, the other is centred on the southern gable and extends only half its depth beyond the building. They are built of dressed stone, the fireplaces lined with red brick, some courses of which are carried across the faces of the walls on the sides of the fireplaces. Some of the beams are pitted with small triangular indentations, evidently to key the plaster.

Page 32

Stuart wears his own hair moderately long, the others wear clerical wigs, with a very slight curl at the edges, and simple in outline. Dissenting ministers abandoned the wig earlier, though Wesley, as still a Church of England clergyman, retained it.

Charles Inglis, 1734-1816, born Ireland. Ordained in England. Assistant rector, Trinity Church, New York, 1765. Loyalist in Revolution. Appointed first bishop of Nova Scotia, 1787. Founded academy at Windsor, N.S., 1788, later King's College.

John Stuart, 1740-1811, born Pennsylvania. Originally a Presbyterian, he joined the Church of England and was ordained 1770. Missionary to Indians on Mohawk River. Chaplain to garrison, Kingston, Upper Canada, 1785, and first incumbent of the church there.

Jacob Mountain, 1749-1825, born England. Appointed first Church of England bishop of Quebec, 1793.

John Ogilvie, 1723-1774. Missionary to the Mohawks, and minister at Albany. Army chaplain at Ticonderoga, Fort Niagara and Montreal, 1759-1760. Assistant rector of Trinity Church, New York, from 1765 until his death.

Page 34

In 1784, a year before his departure, Governor Haldimand began the construction of a new edifice to be used for balls, levees and official receptions. It was situated farther back from the brink of the cliff overlooking the river where stood the earlier building known as the Chateau St. Louis, the residence of the

Governors. One of the curtains of the fort constructed by Frontenac in 1693 served as the exterior wall of the lower storey of the new building, which was not finished until 1787. In December of that year Governor Dorchester and his family took up their residence in this building, while the Chateau St. Louis was occupied by Government offices. Thereafter the Chateau Haldimand, besides being the domicile of the Governor, was the building wherein the official balls, dinners and public receptions took place, as originally intended, its rooms being large and sumptuous, especially its reception hall, which was said to have contained the most beautiful parquet floor in Canada.

Page 36

The church at Clementsport on the slope of South Mountain overlooking Annapolis Basin was built by Dutch and German Loyalists in 1787. Originally Lutheran, it was transferred to the Church of England and consecrated by Bishop Inglis in 1797. The building is solidly constructed with massive timbers, wide and thick boards, hand-split shingles, square-headed hand-wrought nails, crowned by a quaint belfry, and is still in excellent condition. Surrounded by old gravestones and backed by a grove of ancient pine trees, its simple lines and harmonious proportions admirably suggest its antiquity, and the feeling of its period. The church contains a number of relics, and is no longer used as a place of worship, though an anniversary service is held once a year.

Page 38

David F. Thomson's drawing of Surveyors of 1793 appeared in the Calendar of the Toronto Art Students' League for 1897, one of a series of booklets that today are among the rare items of Canadiana. Besides being a vivid and remarkable imaginative reconstruction of a feature of early Canadian life, it is a masterpiece of pen draughtsmanship, suggesting the colour and atmosphere of the wintry forest.

Page 39

Captain John Meares commanded vessels trading between China and the Pacific Coast of North America. They were British ships, but in order to evade the monopoly of the South

Sea Company and the East India Company, which controlled British trade in the Pacific, they sailed under Portuguese colours. In 1788 Meares built and launched a small schooner at Friendly Cove. This vessel, the *North-West America*, was the first ship built on the coast north of Mexico. Spain claimed these waters as part of her territory, and seized this and other vessels belonging to Meares and his associates. Out of this incident arose an international dispute which almost led to war, but which was settled by the treaty known as the Nootka Convention in 1791. See *British Columbia, the Making of a Province*, by F. W. Howay.

Page 41

It is an interesting coincidence that on the same day that Mackenzie saw the Arctic Sea from an island at the mouth of the Mackenzie River, July 14, 1789, the people of Paris attacked and captured the Bastille.

Page 44

Official sanction for the uniform of the Queen's Rangers of Upper Canada is given in the following letter:

War Office, 7 October, 1791.

I have the honour to acquaint you that His Majesty has been pleased to consent that the uniform of the Corps now to be raised under your command shall be green, and of the same pattern as was worn by the late Corps of Queen's Rangers, which you commanded during the late war. I have the honour to be, etc.,

Geo. Yonge

To Col. Simcoe.   (Secretary at War)

Page 47

See note 154 on p. 190, Vol. I, *Picture Gallery of Canadian History*.

Page 49

Francis Gwillim Simcoe, first son and sixth child of Lt.-Governor Simcoe, born Wolford, Devonshire, 1791, and brought to Canada by his parents. Returning with them to England in 1796, he was educated for military life, and entered the army as lieutenant in his twenty-first year. Went with his regiment to Spain, where he was killed in April, 1812, at the storming of Badajoz. At the same siege fell also on April 6th a young Canadian officer of the Royal Engineers, Edouard Alphonse de Salaberry, younger brother of the victor of Chateauguay.

Robert Pilkington (1763-1834), lieutenant in the Royal Engineers, served on Simcoe's staff, 1793-1796. Accompanied him on his journey to Georgian Bay, and made sketches of scenery in that neighbourhood and elsewhere in Upper Canada. Returned to England in 1803, and subsequently became Major-General and Inspector-General of Fortifications.

In the spring of 1794 Simcoe built a summer residence in the woods on the high ground overlooking the River Don, north of the town of York, just beyond the present St. James' Cemetery. The Governor named it Castle Frank after his son. The building was of hewn logs, with four large unbarked pine trunks supporting a pediment or projection of the roof over the front entrance. After the departure of the Simcoes it was occupied occasionally by President Peter Russell and his family; but by 1807 the building was uninhabited and beginning to fall into decay, and finally was accidentally burned in 1829. There are many references to Frank Simcoe and to excursions to Castle Frank in *Mrs. Simcoe's Diary.*

PART TWO

THE SIMCOE FAMILY AT YORK, 1793

C.W.JEFFERYS

EARLY UPPER CANADA PERSONAGES

David W. Smith
Surveyor-General

C.W.J.

William Dummer Powell
Judge Court of King's Bench

William
Jarvis
Provincial Secretary

Hon. Robert Hamilton
Executive Councillor

CUTTING OUT YONGE STREET, 1795

MACKENZIE AT THE PACIFIC

BURLINGTON BEACH

Joseph Brant's House at Burlington. Drawing based on painting by M. Fisher

King's Head Inn

From The Diary of Mrs Simcoe

Burlington Beach, from the south~east

NOVA SCOTIA OFFICIALS

Jonathan Belcher,
1st Chief Justice.
From portrait by Copley.

Samuel Salter
Blowers, C.J.
From portrait by
John P. Drake.

Michael
Wallace.
Treasurer, N.S
From portrait
by R. Field.

Richard Bulkeley, Judge.
From drawing by himself.

Richard John Uniacke, Sr.
Attorney General
From portrait by Rob't. Field.

MORE NOVA SCOTIA OFFICIALS

Sir John Wentworth,
Lieut-Governor 1792
1808

James Boyle
Uniacke.

John Parr, 1725-1791, born Dublin, entered army 1744, Lt.-Colon-
el 1771, Governor of Nova Scotia
during Loyalist migration, Lt.-
Governor N.S. after formation of
Province of New Brunswick.

Sir
Brenton Halliburton, 1775-1860,
born Rhode Island, Judge
1807, Member of Council 1816,
Chief Justice 1833, Knight 1859.
After portrait by A.S. Hoit

OFFICIALS & GOVERNMENT BUILDINGS of UPPER CANADA

Peter Russell, Administrator

William Osgoode, Chief Justice

First Parliament Buildings, 1796-1813.

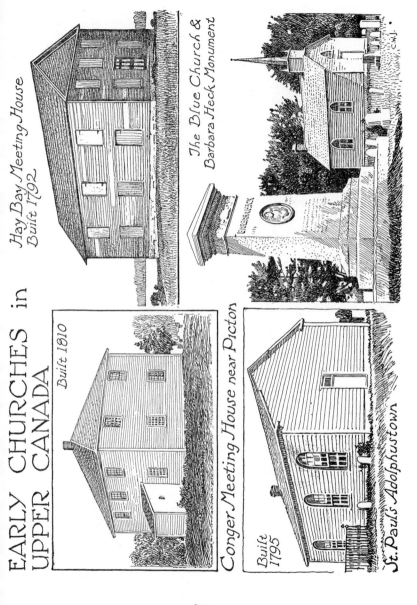

EARLY CHURCHES in UPPER CANADA

Hay Bay Meeting House
Built 1792

The Blue Church &
Barbara Heck Monument

Built 1810

Conger Meeting House near Picton

Built
1795

St. Paul's Adolphustown

CHURCHES } on the RICHELIEU RIVER

St. Antoine
built 1779-81

Door of St. Denis 1792-96

C.W. JEFFERYS

IN OLD MONTREAL.

St.Gabriel Church. Built 1792

House & Store of
Hon.James.McGill

Jacques Cartier
Square Painting
by Georges Delfosse.

Hon.James.McGill

77

PRINCE EDWARD DUKE OF KENT

Rotunda for Band

Only remaining building of the Duke's Estate.

The Prince's Lodge, Bedford Basin near Halifax.

From the painting by J. Weaver, in Province House, Halifax.

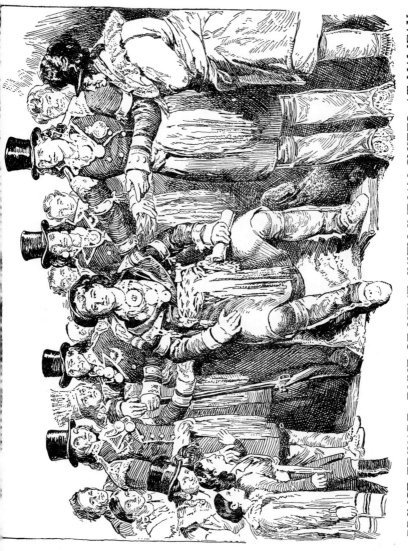

PRINCE EDWARD, DUKE OF KENT, WITH INDIAN CHIEFS, AT HALIFAX

PERSPECTIVE ELEVATION of SAW MILL

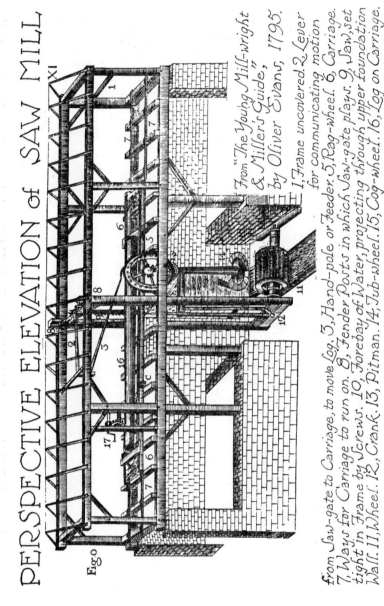

Fig. o

From "The Young Mill-wright & Miller's Guide," by Oliver Evans, 1795.

1, Frame uncolored. 2, Lever for communicating motion from Saw-gate to Carriage, to move Log. 3, Hand-pole or Feeder. 5, Rag-wheel. 6, Carriage. 7, Ways for Carriage to run on. 8, Fender Posts in which Saw-gate plays. 9, Saw, set tight in Frame by Screws. 10, Forebay of Water, projecting through upper foundation Wall. 11, Wheel. 12, Crank. 13, Pitman. 14, Tub-wheel. 15, Cog-wheel. 16, Log on Carriage.

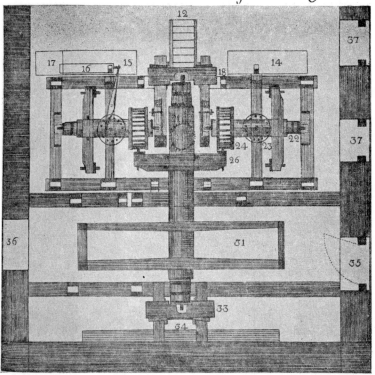

Lower Floor.   12, Step-Ladder from Lower Floor.
14, 15, Meal-troughs & Spouts. 16, Sieve for Corn &
Buckwheat. 17, Box for bran to fall into from Sieve.
18, Head Block for Big Shaft. 21, Shaft of Water-wheel
& Cog-wheel. 22, Little Cog-wheel & Shaft, for Lower
Stones. 23, Trundle. 24, Wallower. 26, Cog-wheel.
31, Water Wheel. 18 feet diameter. 33, Head-block
at Water End. 34, Sill to support End-block.
35, Water-house Door. 36, Hole in Wall for Trunk
to go through. 37, Windows.

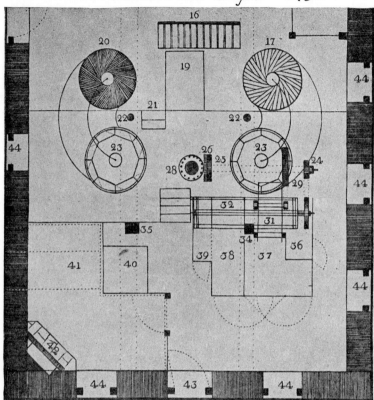

Second Floor. 16, Stairs to 3rd Floor. 17, Stone for Wheat laid off & turned up to be dressed. 19, Stairway. 20, Stone for Corn & Buckwheat laid off. 22, Cranes for lifting Stones. 24, Pulley-wheel to turn Rolling-screen & Fan. 25-26, Shaft & Wheel that turns Screen & Fan. 28, Wheel on upper end of upright shaft. 29, Pulley to turn Fan. 31, Fan. 32, Screen. 34, 35, Posts supporting Girders of 3rd Floor. 36, Room for Tailings. 37, Room for Fannings. 38, Room for Screenings. 39, Room for Dust. 40, Penstock of Water 41, Miller's Office. 42, Fire-place. 43, End Door. 44, Windows

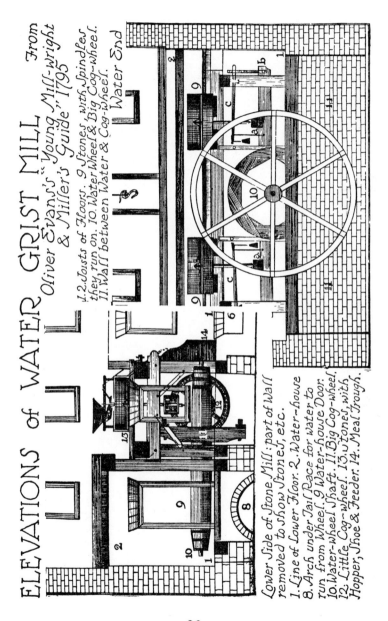

ELEVATIONS of WATER GRIST MILL

From Oliver Evans's "Young Mill-Wright & Miller's Guide" 1795

1,2 Joists of Floors. 9 Stones, with Spindles they run on. 10. Water Wheel & Big Cog-wheel. 11. Wall between Water & Cog-wheel.

Water End

Lower Side of Stone Mill; part of Wall removed to show Stones, etc.
1. Line of Lower Floor. 2. Water-house
8. Arch under Tail Race for water to run from Wheel. 9 Water-house Door.
10. Water-wheel Shaft. 11. Big Cog-wheel.
12. Little Cog-wheel. 13. Stones, with Hopper, Shoe & Feeder. 14. Meal Trough.

GRIST MILL MECHANISM

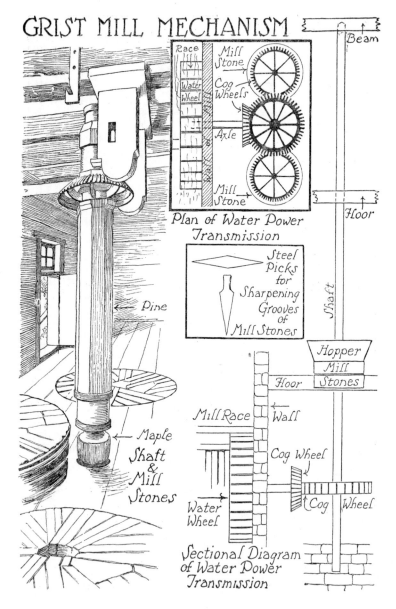

Beam

Race

Mill Stone

Cog Wheels

Water Wheel

Axle

Mill Stone

Plan of Water Power Transmission

Steel Picks for Sharpening Grooves of Mill Stones

Floor

Shaft

Pine

Maple Shaft & Mill Stones

Hopper

Mill Stones

Floor

Mill Race

Wall

Cog Wheel

Water Wheel

Cog Wheel

Sectional Diagram of Water Power Transmission

INTERIOR of GRIST MILL, showing CRANE
for lifting upper stone. Backhouse Mill
near Port Rowan, Ont.

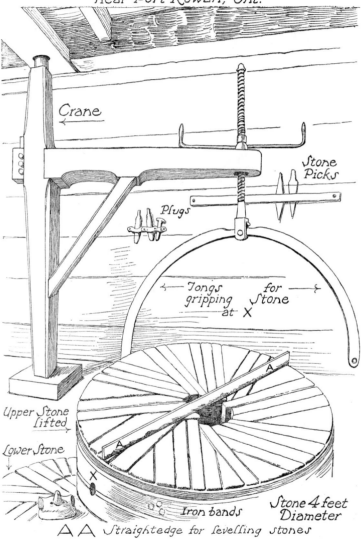

Crane

Stone Picks

Plugs

Tongs gripping at X for Stone

Upper Stone lifted

Lower Stone

A

A

X

Iron bands

Stone 4 feet Diameter

A A Straightedge for levelling stones

The FRENCH ROYALIST COLONY

BOND LAKE

KING TWP.
Boiton
C.Chalus

WHITCHURCH
Saigeon
Farcy TOWNSHIP

VAUGHAN T.P.
Comte de
Chalus
St.George
Farcy
Puisaye
C.Chalus
Marchand
Le Bugle
Renoux
Saigeon

MARKHAM TWP.
Farcy
St. George
Furon
Boiton
Letourneau
Vicomte Chalus
Marseuil

Fauchard

Vicomte de
Chalus

Comte de
Chalus

Comte
de
Puisaye

ORANGE HOME
(TO-DAY)

YONGE STREET

ELGIN MILLS

*Location of
the Yonge Street Settlement*

Comte
Joseph de Puisaye

Puisaye's House on the Niagara River

86

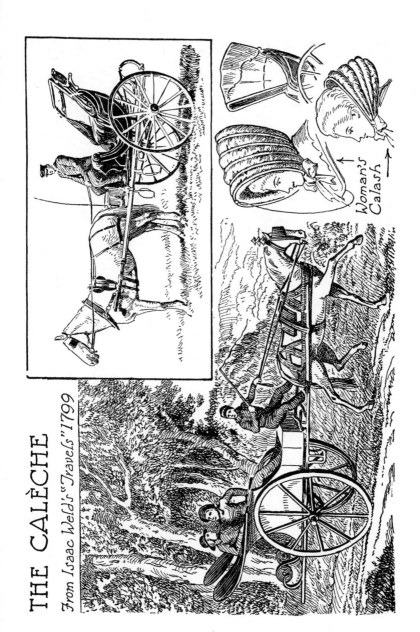

Woman's Calash

THE CALÈCHE

From Isaac Weld's "Travels" 1799

87

TRAVELLER'S · LUGGAGE

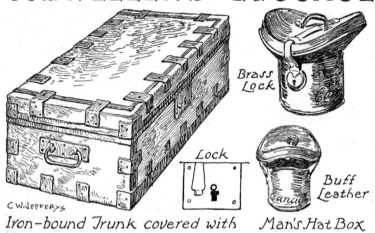

C.W.JEFFERYS

Brass Lock

Lock

Buff Leather

Iron-bound Trunk covered with Calf-skin. In Church at Clementsport, N.S.

Man's Hat Box

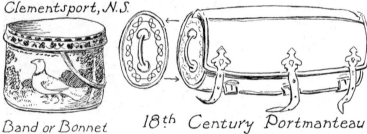

Band or Bonnet Box

18ᵗʰ Century Portmanteau

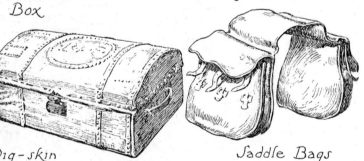

Pig-skin Trunk studded with Brass Nails

Saddle Bags

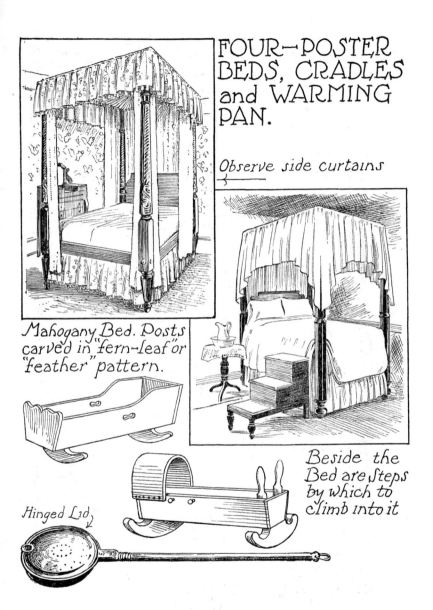

FOUR-POSTER BEDS, CRADLES and WARMING PAN.

Observe side curtains

Mahogany Bed. Posts carved in "fern-leaf" or "feather" pattern.

Beside the Bed are steps by which to climb into it

Hinged Lid

BED ROOM FURNITURE

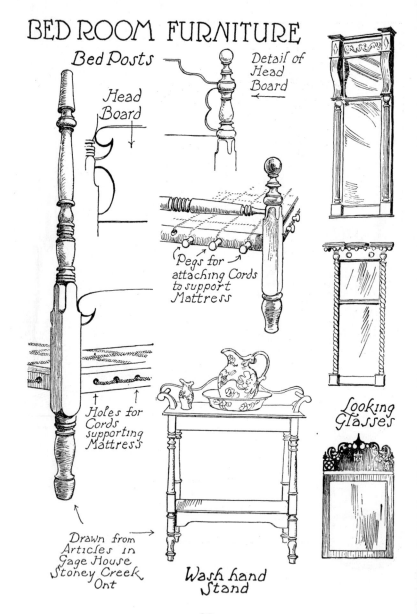

Bed Posts

Head Board

Detail of Head Board

Pegs for attaching Cords to support Mattress

Holes for Cords supporting Mattress

Drawn from Articles in Gage House Stoney Creek Ont

Wash hand Stand

Looking Glasses

90

ARTICLES of MILITARY EQUIPMENT

Gilt

Gorget of Col. Fanning King's American Regiment 1776-1783

In Fort Ticonderoga Museum

Silver

Gorget 1770-1796

Lieutenant of Infantry 1796 with Gorget & Single Epaulette

Cross Belt

Right

Left

Officer's Epaulette

22½ inches

GR

2nd West Batl. Militia

Belt Plate

Artillery Epaulettes

16 inches

Drum carried by Enoch Goodwin, Westmoreland Militia, N.B. 1776. In Beausejour Museum

Cartridge Box

C.W.J.

Bayonet Scabbard

Powder Horns used by Militia 1776 +

FELLING AXES

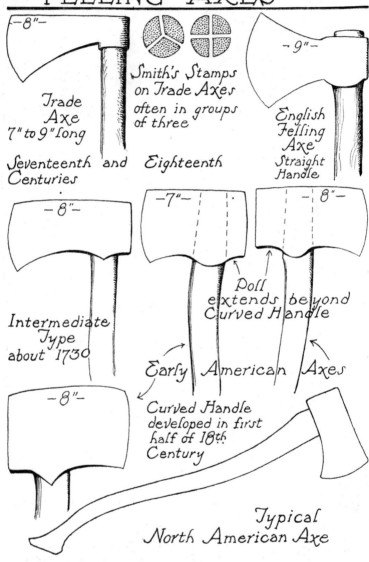

—8"—

Trade
Axe
7" to 9" Long

Seventeenth and
Centuries

Smith's Stamps
on Trade Axes
often in groups
of three

Eighteenth

—9"—

English
Felling
Axe
Straight
Handle

—8"—

Intermediate
Type
about 1730

—7"—

—8"—

Poll
extends beyond
Curved Handle

Early American Axes

Curved Handle
developed in first
half of 18th
Century

—8"—

Typical
North American Axe

HEWING AXES & ADZES

Wedge

Curved Helve

Outer side

Eye

Inner side ↑

Wedge ↑ Poll ↑ Blade ↑

Diagram of Off-set Helve

Chisel edge

Knife-edged Broad Axes

—8½"—

—9"—

—8"—

—7"—

—9½"—

—9½"—

Hewing   Axe   Patterns

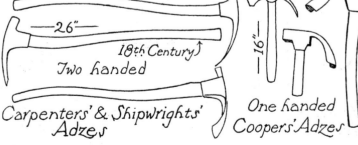

—26"—

18th Century ↑

Two handed

Carpenters' & Shipwrights' Adzes

—16"—

One handed Coopers' Adzes

HATCHETS

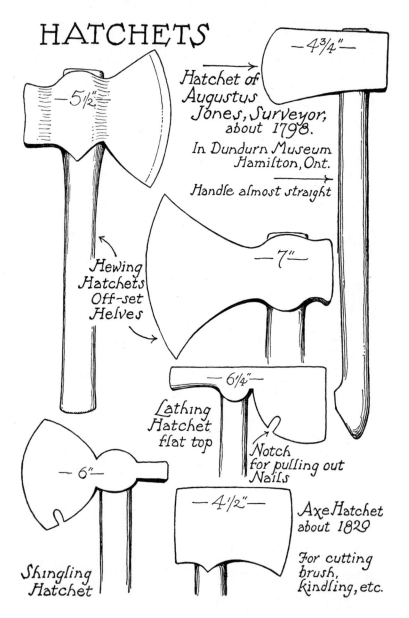

—5½"—

—4¾"—

Hatchet of
Augustus
Jones, Surveyor,
about 1798.

In Dundurn Museum
Hamilton, Ont.

Handle almost straight

Hewing
Hatchets
Off-set
Helves

—7"—

—6¼"—

Lathing
Hatchet
flat top

Notch
for pulling out
Nails

—6"—

—4½"—

Axe Hatchet
about 1829

Shingling
Hatchet

For cutting
brush,
kindling, etc.

94

RAIL SPLITTER.

Courtesy of Dr W Perkins Buff K C

FENCE VIEWERS.

C.W.JEFFERYS

Fence Viewers

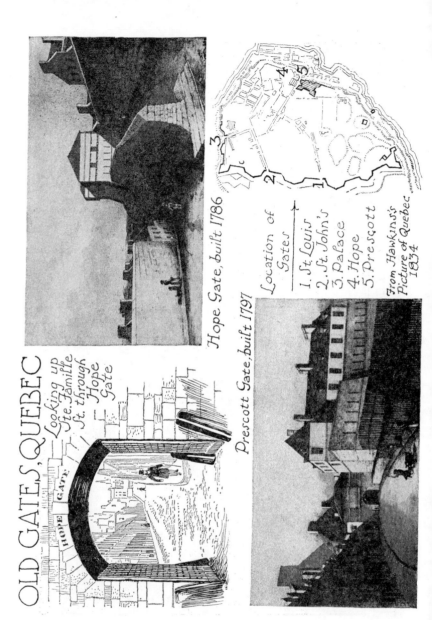

OLD GATES, QUEBEC

Looking up Ste. Famille St. through Hope Gate

HOPE GATE

Hope Gate, built 1786

Prescott Gate, built 1797

Location of Gates

1. St. Louis
2. St. John's
3. Palace
4. Hope
5. Prescott

From Hawkins's Picture of Quebec 1834

96

OLD GATES OF QUEBEC

*From Lithographs by Bourne, in
Hawkins's Picture of Quebec,
published 1834*
*Drawn on stone by Sproule, after
sketches by A.J.Russell.*

Palace Gate
built 1750
rebuilt 1831

St. John's Gate, originally built 1693

St. Louis Gate, originally built 1693

All these gates were torn down in 1871

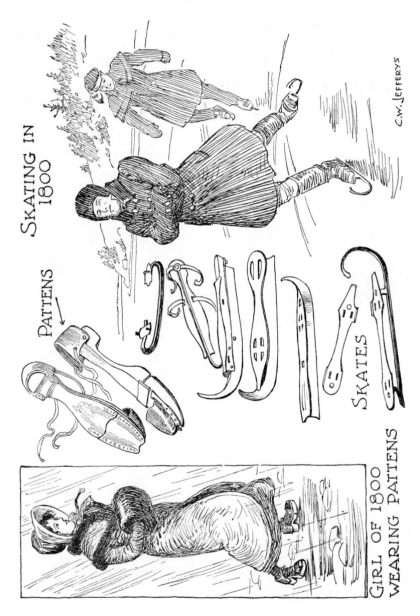

SKATING IN 1800

PATTENS

SKATES

GIRL OF 1800 WEARING PATTENS

C.W. JEFFERYS

JOHN JEWITT, CAPTIVE OF CHIEF MAQUINA AT
NOOTKA, 1803

YORK GARRISON · · UPPER CANADA

Sketch by Mrs. Simcoe Showing first Houses and Magazine on Shore 1796
From Diary

Plan of Fort 1816

York Barracks, May, 1804.

LIGHTHOUSE & SIGNAL STATION

Toronto Island Lighthouse

Built 1808. Upper part added 1832. Height 82 feet. From Robertson's Landmarks of Toronto.

Telegraph Signal on Lake Ontario

C.W.JEFFERYS

YORK 1804
KINGSTON 1828

Part of York.

From water colour in the W.H. Coverdale Collection, by Mrs E.F. Hale, wife of a Government official. View looking east shows in distance Legislative Buildings & Block House.

Kingston from Fort Henry.

From aquatint by J Gleadah, after J Grey. View shows warships of 1812, dismasted & covered in, & "stone frigate," building still used by Royal Military College

Stone Frigate

THE FIRST RAFT ON THE OTTAWA, 1806

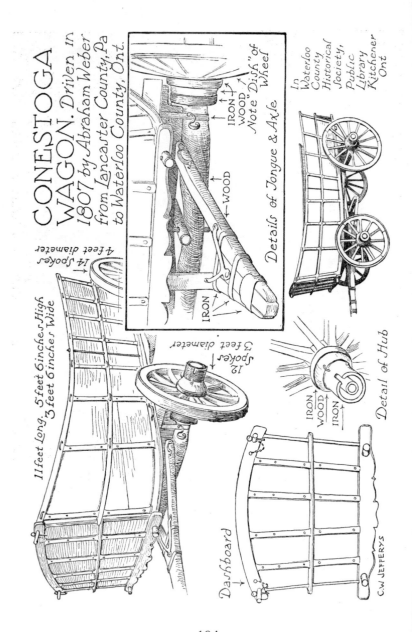

CONESTOGA WAGON. Driven in 1807 by Abraham Weber from Lancaster County, Pa to Waterloo County, Ont.

In Waterloo County Historical Society, Public Library Kitchener Ont

Details of Tongue & Axle

IRON
WOOD
Note "Dish" of Wheel

WOOD

IRON

14 Spokes 4 feet diameter

11 feet Long, 5 feet 6 inches High 3 feet 6 inches Wide

12 Spokes 3 feet diameter

IRON
WOOD
IRON

Detail of Hub

Dashboard

C.W. JEFFERYS

104

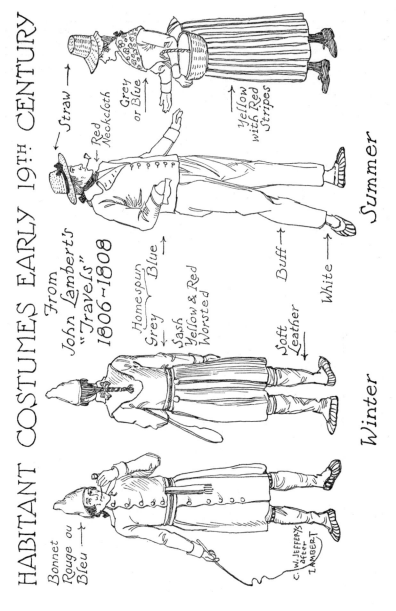

HABITANT COSTUMES EARLY 19TH CENTURY

From John Lambert's "Travels" 1806~1808

Bonnet Rouge ou Bleu →

Straw →

Red Neckcloth

Grey or Blue

Yellow with Red Stripes

Homespun Grey Blue →

Sash Yellow & Red Worsted

Soft Leather →

Buff →

White →

Winter

Summer

C. W. JEFFERYS after LAMBERT

WINTER COSTUMES *From John Lambert's "Travels" 1806~1808*

Priest →

Officer ←

INDIAN COSTUMES about 1807

From G. Heriot's "Travels"

ROUND DANCE OF THE CANADIANS

From drawing by George Heriot, in his "Travels."

FRENCH CANADIAN DANCE

From drawing by George Heriot, in his "Travels."

SIMON FRASER DESCENDING THE FRASER RIVER, 1808

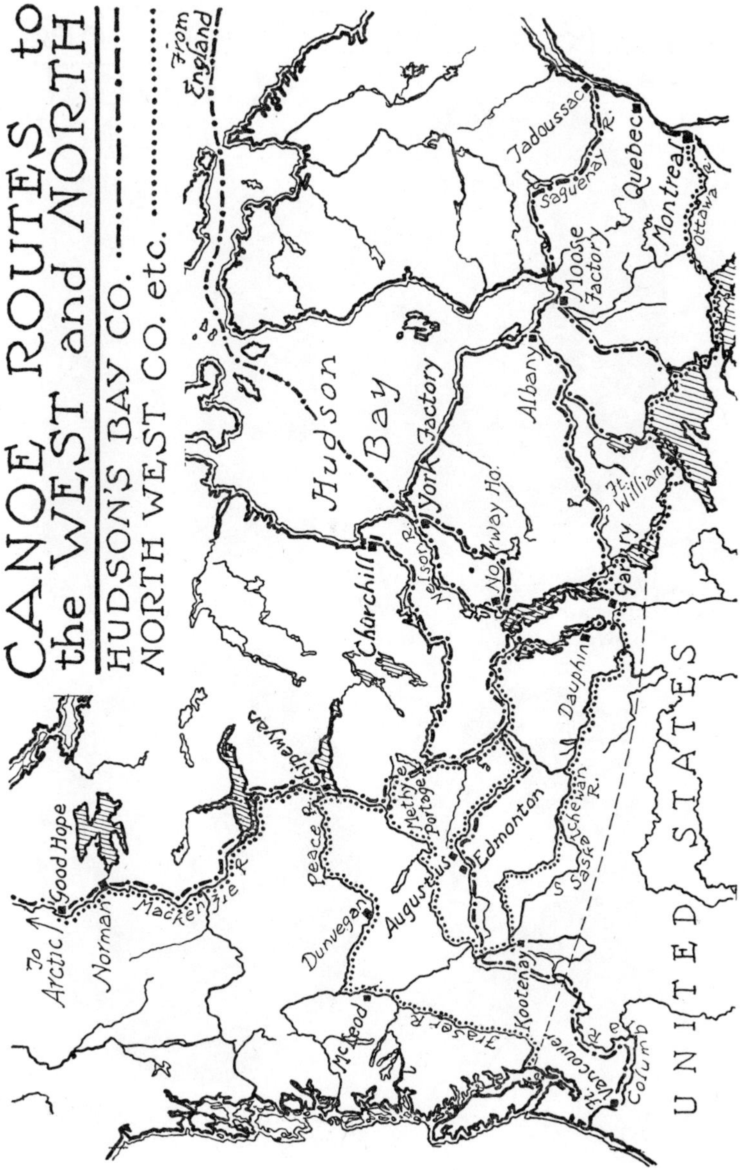

CANOE ROUTES to the WEST and NORTH

HUDSON'S BAY CO. ....
NORTH WEST CO. etc. ....
From England

To Arctic
Good Hope
Norman
Mackenzie R.
Peace R.
Athabasca R.
McLeod
Fraser R.
Dunvegan
Methye Portage
Augustus Portage
Kootenay
Vancouver
Columbia R.
Edmonton
S. Saskn. R.
Dauphin
Churchill
Nelson R.
York Factory
Norway Ho.
Fort William
Albany
Moose Factory
Jadoussac
Saguenay R.
Quebec
Montreal
Ottawa R.
Hudson Bay

UNITED STATES

111

Vol. II.-5

FUR TRADERS of the NORTH WEST COMPANY

Simon McTavish
*From painting in McCord
Museum, Montreal*

Joseph Frobisher

Simon Fraser

William McGillivray
Painting in McCord Museum

HOUSES of the FUR TRADERS
MONTREAL

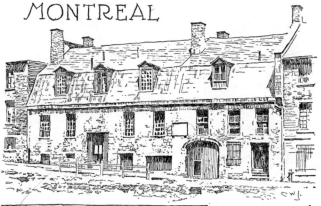

← *Left* and *Top.↑ House
on St. Jean Baptiste
Street, occupied by
Simon Mc.Tavish
1786 ~ 1804.*

Courtesy of E.Z. Massicotte

*Corner of
St. Thérèse and
Vaudreuil Streets,
North West Co.
storehouse 1815.*

X *Lodging and
storehouse of John
Jacob Astor.*

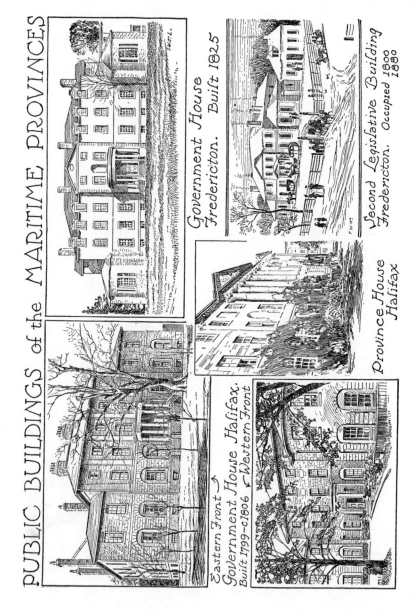

PUBLIC BUILDINGS of the MARITIME PROVINCES

Government House
Fredericton. Built 1825

Second Legislative Building
Fredericton. Occupied 1800
1880

Province House
Halifax

Eastern Front ↑
Government House Halifax.
Built 1799–c1806 ←Western Front

114

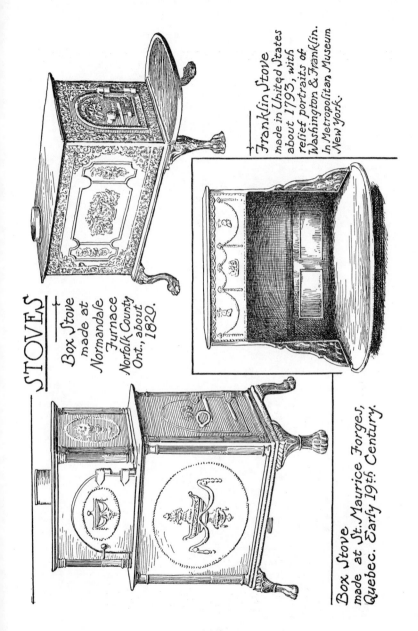

STOVES

Box Stove
made at
Normandale
Furnace
Norfolk County
Ont., about
1820.

Franklin Stove
made in United States
about 1793, with
relief portraits of
Washington & Franklin.
In Metropolitan Museum
New York.

Box Stove
made at St. Maurice Forges,
Quebec. Early 19th Century.

115

MILITIA TRAINING ON THE KING'S BIRTHDAY

C.W.JEFFERYS

NOTES ON PART TWO

Page 67

On August 23rd, 1793, Simcoe ordered that the name of Toronto should be changed to York, in honour of the success of the Duke of York against the French in Holland.

Mrs. Simcoe's *Diary* says, "There was a party of Ojibway Indians here, who appeared much pleased with the firing."—a salute of 21 guns to celebrate the occasion. "One of them took Francis in his arms, and was much pleased to find the child not afraid, but delighted with the sound."

The illustration shows Mrs. Simcoe's hound, "Trojan," who once disgraced himself, as she says, by tearing in pieces a map of Canada which she had drawn. In the background is shown the "canvas house," in which the Simcoes lived. This was a large tent which had been used by Captain Cook in his South Sea expedition, and which Simcoe had bought in London at the sale of the explorer's effects. It was set up on the high ground east of Garrison Creek, at the foot of the present Bathurst Street, Toronto.

Page 68

David W. Smith (1764-1837), son of Lieutenant-Colonel John Smith, of the 5th Regiment, Northumberland Fusiliers, who was commandant of Fort Niagara. Son was officer in the same regiment. Member and Speaker of House of Assembly. Appointed Surveyor-General, Upper Canada, 1792. Returned to England, 1802. Became manager of Duke of Northumberland's estates. Created Baronet, 1821. His house at Newark, built about 1793, was one of the finest in the province at that period. The Toronto Public Library acquired in England a large collection of his papers, which contain much valuable material on early Upper Canada.

William Dummer Powell, born in Massachusetts, educated in England and Holland. Returning to Boston, 1772, he came thence to Canada, where he was admitted to practise law. Later became judge and was Chief-Justice, 1816-1825. Prominent in the province during its early years. See monograph on him by His Honour Judge W. R. Riddell, the authority on the legal history of Upper Canada.

William Jarvis (1756-1817), born in Connecticut. Cornet in Queen's Rangers, and served in Revolutionary War. Came to Upper Canada as Secretary and Registrar of the province. His family, descendants and connections were prominent in public affairs for many years.

Hon. Robert Hamilton (1750-1809), born in Scotland, established himself at Queenston soon after the Revolutionary War. He and Hon. Richard Cartwright at Kingston were the principal merchants in early Upper Canada. Member of the Land Board and of the Executive Council. Much correspondence relating to business is contained in the *Cartwright Papers* in the Douglas Library, Queen's University, Kingston. See also paper on the Hamilton family, by H. F. Gardiner, in Vol. VIII, *Ontario Historical Society, Papers and Records*.

Note that the costumes and hair-dressing of Smith and Jarvis are of an earlier date than those of Powell and Hamilton: the former wear wigs, the latter their own hair   The wig began to go out of fashion about the time of the French Revolution, though it was retained by many elderly men until the early years of the nineteenth century.

Page 70

Mackenzie in his *Journey* speaks of having a "hanger," a short sword, convenient for travelling in rough country, similar to that carried by Wolfe, as shown in the drawing in Vol. I, p. 242, depicting him at the Battle of the Plains.

Page 72

Hon. Jonathan Belcher (1710-1776), born Boston, son of the Governor of Massachusetts and of New Jersey. Chief Justice, 1754; and Lieutenant-Governor, 1761-1763, of Nova Scotia. Buried in St. Paul's Church, Halifax.

Hon. Samuel Salter Blowers, born Boston, 1742, died Halifax, aged one hundred years. Judge in Rhode Island. Arrived in Halifax, 1783. Was successively Attorney-General, Member of House of Assembly and Legislative Council, Chief Justice, 1797, and Master of the Rolls.

Hon. Richard Bulkeley (1717-1800), born in Ireland. came to Halifax with Cornwallis, 1749. Was Secretary, and later, Administrator of the Province, and held various judicial positions.

Hon. Richard John Uniacke, Sr., born Ireland, 1753, died Mount Uniacke, N.S., 1830, buried in St. Paul's, Halifax. Settled in Nova Scotia, 1774, Speaker of House of Assembly and Attorney-General. The portrait by Field was painted in 1811.

Michael Wallace was administrator at various times from 1818 to 1830.

The portraits of the judges are in the Court House at Halifax.

Pages 72 and 73

John Poad Drake (1794-1883): born in England; came to Halifax 1819, painted full-length portrait of Chief Justice S. S. Blowers, apparently the only one painted in Halifax. Went to Montreal, where he painted an altar-piece for one of the churches, and later went to New York, where he exhibited a painting of Napoleon on board the *Bellerophon*, a scene which he had witnessed in Plymouth Sound in 1815. Returned to England, where he died in Cornwall.

Robert Field, born Gloucester, England, about 1770. Came to America about 1792, and worked in New York, Philadelphia, Washington and Boston until 1808, when he settled in Halifax until his death in 1819. In the United States his work was mostly in miniature, though he painted some portraits in oil, and also executed several engravings. In Nova Scotia most of his portraits were oil paintings. Among his sitters were Sir John Wentworth, Sir John Coape Sherbrooke, Sir George Prevost and Bishop Inglis. He is probably the most distinguished of the early portrait painters of the Maritime Provinces.

Albert Gallatin Hoit, or Hoyt (1809-1856), born in New Hampshire, worked for a time in Boston. He visited Saint John, N.B., and later, about 1840, Halifax, N.S., where he painted the full-length portrait of Sir Brenton Halliburton, and possibly some others.

The notes on these artists are from data kindly supplied by Mr. William Colgate.

Page 74

Observe that Russell and Osgoode wear their own hair, though powdered and arranged in a fashion somewhat resembling a wig; and that the Chief Justice does not wear a full-bottomed wig nor robes, such as appear in the portraits of early Nova Scotia judges. These were never worn by lawyers or judges in Upper Canada. Information given by His Honour Judge W. R. Riddell.

The first Legislative Buildings in York were situated at the lower end of the present Berkeley Street. They were burned by the Americans during the occupancy of York in April, 1813.

Page 76

Most of the early Quebec churches existing today were built during the period from about 1770 to 1825. This was evidently a time of prosperity for the people of Lower Canada, as shown by the numerous and sumptuously furnished churches of this date. The parish records give details of the money paid to architects and sculptors, in addition to the labour and materials supplied by the parishioners.

The architectural style of these churches was classic, that of the late Renaissance, known as Baroque. It is interesting to compare them with those of Mexico and California, built about the same time and designed in the same style. The southern churches, outside and within, were more ornate and florid. Those of Quebec, in their exterior decoration, were plainer, more restrained, in conformity with their northern climatic conditions. Their charm consists in their pleasing proportions, their union of dignity and grace, and their harmony with their landscape setting. The Quebec craftsmen lavished their decorative skill on the interiors, in wood carving, plaster work on altars, pulpits, ceilings, sacristry doors, etc., some examples of which are shown in these pages.

Information on these craftsmen and their work is to be found in books, monographs and articles by Marius Barbeau, Emile Vaillancourt Ramsay Traquair, Prof. E. R. Adair, and Gerard Morisset.

Page 77

The corner stone of the Nelson monument was laid in 1809. Near it was the pillory where criminals were exposed with a label on their breasts stating the nature of their offence. Here, too, prisoners convicted of larceny were punished by being tied to a cannon near the column and given 39 lashes on the naked back.

St. Gabriel Church was supported by members of the North-West Company and other fur-traders, who were Scotch Presbyterians.

Page 79

By the time covered in this volume the Indians, especially in the settled parts of Canada, had long been in contact with the whites. Their way of life in consequence had been considerably modified by European influences. Their primitive tools of bone, wood and stone had been displaced by steel knives and tomahawks, guns, needles and thread, etc.; fur robes and deer skins were supplemented by cloth and blankets; porcupine quills and moosehair embroidery were largely discarded for beads and silver ornaments and trade wampum of white manufacture.

Not only the native materials and technique were affected by European influence: their aboriginal designs, mostly geometrical, also included imitations of the patterns of flowered textile fabrics brought by traders. French nuns taught Indian girls sewing and embroidery in which floral motives were copied.

Undoubtedly these changes began at a very early period of white contact. It is unwise to be dogmatic concerning this, since detailed information is vague and scanty, and the dates of many specimens of Indian work in museums are uncertain. How much of this Indian handcraft is indigenous and aboriginal in design, and how much is modified by European influences is debatable, and there is much divergence of opinion among ethnologists on this question. Only when the materials used are of European manufacture, as beads, thread, and so forth, can we be certain that articles date from the coming of white people.

It is possible that the Indians used formalized floral designs supplied by native plants: the A'gonkian double-curve motive may well have been suggested by waves and wind ripples. Native ingenuity fashioned many necessary articles, and, as the student of the development of arts and crafts knows, peoples widely separated and never in contact evolve designs and shape objects that are remarkably similar in appearance. It has been asserted that the making of birch-bark containers was taught by the French to the Indians. But it seems not unreasonable to suppose that the aboriginal mind that could conceive and fashion

121

the canoe, a masterpiece of Indian handcraft, was capable of manufacturing a vessel which would keep water *in*, no less than one which would keep water *out*.

Since, however, the purpose of these volumes is to depict and describe the life of the country within historic times, the question of pre-European Indian culture is beyond their scope, and need not be further considered. It will suffice perhaps to say that in the more remote portions of the country, where only an occasional explorer, or a few traders had penetrated, Indian life retained more of its primitive and indigenous features than in those districts where white settlement was well established.

The European new-comers, in turn, were influenced by their contact with the Indians, and soon realized the suitability of many of their inventions to the conditions of the wilderness and early settlement. They adopted the snowshoe, the canoe, the toboggan, and various articles of costume, some of which are still in use on the frontiers of civilization today.

For our knowledge of primitive Indian life we must depend largely upon the descriptions and the drawings of early eye-witnesses, in books of travel and exploration. Indeed, these may be said to be our only sources of information concerning the earliest periods of white and Indian contact, accurate, or incorrect, or provokingly vague in detail as they may be. On the whole these observers strike one as being trustworthy. Many of them, such as the early missionary priests, were highly intelligent, well-educated men, versed in the science of their time. They interpreted the facts they observed in accordance with their prejudices, and with the limitations of the knowledge available at their time; but the facts themselves, for the most part, bear the stamp of authenticity. The bibliography includes the most important works dealing with the subject; but much incidental material may be found in many books concerning the general life of the time. Indeed, scarcely a book on Canada published during this period is without some reference to Indian conditions. Quotations from some of these works are given in the notes.

This picture is copied from a lithograph by H. Linch, after a painting by H. D. Thielcke. It shows the official or gala costume worn by Canadian Indian chiefs about 1796. Tall "plug" hats, decorated with ostrich feathers, braided frock coats with brass

122

or silver buttons, medals and gorgets were given by the British Government, as insignia of their office, to the chiefs, especially among the eastern tribes, throughout the greater part of the nineteenth century. The arm bands were articles of trade silver, manufactured mainly in Montreal. Moccasins were about the only articles of their clothing of native design and manufacture.

Page 85

The beautifully carpentered crane resembles an engraving in Oliver Evans's *Young Mill-wright's Guide*, but is more elegant in design. In order to keep the mill-stones sharp, it was necessary, from time to time, to deepen the furrows and dress the surface afresh. By means of the upright iron screw and the grappling tongs the crane was used to lift and turn over the upper stone. The furrows were then deepened by steel picks. To test the levels of the stones and ensure equal contact, a wooden bar whose edge was smeared with red earth moistened with water was drawn across their surfaces. The higher parts where the red smear was seen were then dressed off until the whole surface was perfectly level.

Page 86

In 1797 Count Joseph de Puisaye, a refugee from the French Revolution, laid a plan before the British Government for the settlement of a number of French Royalist émigrés on lands to be granted to them in Canada. The Government agreed to the proposal, and in the summer of 1798 a party under the leadership of Puisaye set sail from Portsmouth. They arrived at Quebec early in October, and thence were transported, partly by land and partly in batteaux, to Kingston. Here they spent the winter, while Puisaye proceeded to York, to consult with President Peter Russell, who had been notified earlier by the British Government of the project. Russell and the Executive Council selected a location for the colony on Yonge Street, in the townships of Markham, Vaughan, Whitchurch and King. The situation was chosen as "being equally distant from the French of Detroit and Lower Canada, and near enough to the seat of Government both to give assistance to them and to keep an eye on them"—a consideration which indicates the suspicion with which all true Britons then regarded Frenchmen.

Early next spring the émigrés arrived, and began the difficult task of trying to make homes for themselves in the forest. It was a task for which they were ill-fitted, most of them being noblemen and former officers of the Royal Army, unaccustomed to the hard physical labour of pioneer life. The colony, after a few years of feeble existence, was abandoned, most of the émigrés returning to Europe.

One of them, however, Quetton St. George, became a successful trader, and remained in Canada until the downfall of Napoleon, when he too returned to France. At the time of his departure he was probably the most prosperous merchant in Upper Canada, with establishments extending from Detroit to the neighbourhood of Orillia, and the owner of considerable landed property. His son, born in France after his father's return, later came to Canada and settled on his property near Wilcox Lake, where he built a handsome house, and laid out extensive grounds. The house was destroyed by fire after his death, but a noble avenue of pine trees and several of the hedges he planted still remain. He is buried in the graveyard of the church at Oak Ridges.

Puisaye, after seeing his followers established on Yonge Street, acquired land on the Niagara River, where part of his house is still standing. Here he lived, in some state, until 1801, when he returned to England, where he remained for the rest of his life. Much of his correspondence while in Canada is preserved in the papers of Hon. Richard Cartwright, who was his business agent, in the Library of Queen's University, Kingston.

See *A Colony of Émigrés in Canada, 1798-1816*, by Lucy E. Textor, Ph.D., University of Toronto Studies in History, 1905. Also *Les Ecclésiastiques et Les Royalistes Français*, by N. E. Dionne.

Page 87

The Calèche was a two-wheeled vehicle in use in Lower Canada, similar to the "one-hoss shay," or chaise of New England with the addition of a seat in front for the driver. It had a hood that could be raised or lowered.

Toward the end of the eighteenth century a head-dress for women known as a Calash came into use, which took its name from its resemblance to the hood of the vehicle. It was made of a frame of wire or whale-bone hoops encircling the head and hinged together at the bottom so that it could be thrown back if desired. It was covered with oiled silk or other waterproof textile material. For wear in cold weather it was padded inside with wool, fur, or eider-down. Sometimes it was provided with a cord attached to the top of the front by which it could be pulled forward.

Page 89

Bedsteads were furnished with a canopy, called a tester, and side curtains which could be drawn close to keep out draughts and "night air," which was thought to be harmful to health. Thick feather mattresses often built the bed so high that steps were required to enable the sleeper to get into it. A long-handled warming pan—a copper or brass dish in which was placed glowing charcoal or embers from the fireplace—was used to warm the sheets before retiring. Many bedrooms were unheated, though some had small open fireplaces. Beds such as those illustrated were used only by a few well-to-do settlers who brought them from their earlier homes in Great Britain or the American colonies, or acquired them at a later period when the pioneers had reached some prosperity.

Page 90

Much of the pioneer furniture was home-made, in spells of leisure on rainy days and in winter, or by a neighbouring carpenter. The woods most in use were birch, cherry, black walnut, basswood and maple. Black walnut was very popular until the latter half of the eighteenth century, when it was superseded by mahogany in the houses of fashionable society. Patrick Campbell says: "Maple and black clouded birch of New Brunswick and black walnut of Upper Canada are equal for household furnishing and furniture to any in the world. In the Governor's house, the Judge's house, and others, I have seen most beautiful specimens. Yet so prevalent is custom and the

125

desire of emulation the bane of society, that many gentlemen, who cannot well afford it, have mahogany furniture in abundance, and despise what can be got at their door."

Page 92

This page is planned to show the changes in the shape of the axe from the European tool of the first settlers on this continent to the typical North American axe of the nineteenth century. Many of the early axes were of European manufacture, but apparently almost from the beginning those which were made for this continent were of a pattern somewhat different from most of those in use in the home lands. The type known as the trade axe or hatchet, probably originating in France, was introduced into Canada at an early date, and spread thence throughout North America. From it possibly has developed the special shape peculiar to this continent.

Its characteristic features are, first, the increasing projection of the poll or butt of the axe beyond the helve, to give added weight and power to its drive; second, the flattening of its upper border and the comparatively narrow flare of its blade in contrast to the European type and to the hewing or smoothing axe; and third, the substitution of a curving handle for the almost straight European handle.

Local blacksmiths soon began to modify the shape of the axes sent out, and to forge axes themselves, in accordance with their own ideas and the suggestions of their pioneer customers. Hence there were many variations of shape: the drawings illustrate the general tendency of the evolution of the axe in this country. These blacksmith axes were made by folding together the tapering ends of a block of iron, heated so as to be malleable. Into these ends was inserted a strip of steel for the blade, and the whole then welded together. The middle portion, thick enough to provide for the projecting poll, was fitted over a handle pattern to form an oval or egg-shaped eye. The helves were generally made of hickory, or sometimes of white oak or ash.

It is impossible to fix precise dates for these changes; but we know that in the first half of the eighteenth century the St. Maurice Forges at Three Rivers were turning out axes. By the time of the founding of Halifax, 1749, the axe of this continent had acquired its peculiar characteristics. This we may infer from a letter of Governor Cornwallis, in which he states that such slow progress had been made in tree felling by his settlers with their European axes that he had employed Massachusetts men with their American axes as being more rapid and efficient.

Emigrants continued to bring with them European axes long after the North American implement had been developed. According to Canniff Old World axes were supplied by the British Government to the Loyalists and other early settlers. These were often of inferior quality, and their shape was unsuited to pioneer needs, being really short-handled ship axes, intended for quite different uses than chopping trees and clearing land. Even as late as the settlement of the Lake Simcoe region, according to an article in the Toronto *Globe* in 1885, "English axes with straight handles were used by the pioneers at Big Bay Point, and a Yankee pedler tried to persuade them of the superior usefulness of axes with crooked handles."

Not only was the shape of the European axe less suitable for the rapid felling of the huge trees of the North American forest: its steel was not tempered to the severe cold of the Canadian winter, when most of the chopping was done. A letter of Butler in 1781. speaking of the situation of the Niagara Loyalist settlers, says, "A Smith will be requisite for mending and making Plow Shares, Hoes and Axes." Simcoe, in September, 1793, writes, "Axes should be made of the best materials, and of the shape and size of the pattern sent. The axe will weigh rather more than 5 pounds. Particular attention must be given to tempering the steel, without which the axe will be of no value, as in the case of those already sent over. . . . Those made in America, though not so neatly fabricated, are of infinitely more value to the persons who use them. It is customary with the manufacturers in America to warrant the quality of the tools they make for 6 months, and to take back or replace those that are found insufficient." The breaking of an axe was a tragedy to the settler isolated in the depths of the backwoods. In the letters and reports of George Simpson of the Hudson's Bay Company in 1820-1821 we find several references to this subject: "Our English Hatchets are so badly tempered that they do not stand the severity of the Frost, are as brittle as Glass, . . . those of Canadian manufacture are found to answer much better in this country." "The axes are of the worst materials and badly tempered, they should be manufactured of the best Swedish Iron and German Steel and tempered with great care. . . They are most required when the Thermometer is about 50 degrees below Zero. . . . The Indians are aware of their inferior quality and invariably reserve a few Skins to obtain a supply from the North West Coy. The small sized hatchets are too large and round in the Eye."

For sharpening the axe the grindstone was used in the settlements, or wherever its transportation was possible; but the isolated pioneer was dependent upon a small home-made whetstone when he was not within easy distance of a grindstone. In the Hudson's Bay Company's territory iron files were used for this purpose.

The history of the evolution of the axe, especially in its relation to Canada, has yet to be written; but much useful information may be gathered from *Ancient Carpenters' Tools*, by H. C. Mercer, the Bucks County Historical Society, Doylestown, Pa. This contains many illustrations, and is the most complete work on the subject of American wood-working tools with which I am acquainted. Some excellent illustrations are to be found in Thoreau MacDonald's booklet, *Some Tools of the Pioneers* published by him in Toronto, 1936.

Page 93

The Hewing Axe was used by lumbermen for squaring timbers for rafting and stowage in vessels, and by carpenters for smoothing beams, planks and rafters. For these purposes the inner or *left* side of the axe in contact with the timber was straight and level. The handle was bent outward to the right so that the knuckles of the workman's hands should clear the log.

The log was placed about knee-high on cross beams laid on the ground. The bark was chopped off to roughly square the log. The required width was marked at the ends and small spikes driven in Between these spikes was stretched a stout line, chalked with red or black crayon. The hewer, standing on the log, midway of its length, lifted the cord some inches above the log, and when it was drawn taut, released the cord, which snapped back and marked a straight line on the timber. Then, standing on the ground with the log close to his leg, and holding the axe with both hands, he hewed downwards diagonally across the grain. He took care to "hew to the line" evenly and smoothly, so that the timbers should be of uniform dimensions and smooth surfaced. This was necessary in order that they might fit snugly together in the hold of the ship, and not shift with its rolling in the Atlantic billows on the voyage to Europe.

Some broad axes were made with the *right* side straight. These were for left-handed hewers. When such workmen were employed it was possible for two sides of the log to be hewn at the same time, the two hewers working from opposite ends. Left-handed hewers were paid higher wages because of the time saved.

The Adze was used for shaping beams and rafters, for levelling and smoothing floor planks and for excavating log troughs and dug-out canoes. The edge of the blade was generally straight, though sometimes a curved or saucer-edged blade was used to produce a rippled surface which gave a pleasing play of light and shade along the smooth surface of the beam or plank. These saucer-edged adzes had to be sharpened by a file or whetstone, it being impossible to apply them to a grindstone for this purpose.

The Cooper's Adze was used for hewing down barrel staves as well as for shaping and finishing wooden bowls and troughs. As will be seen by the drawings, it was more deeply curved downward and also more often saucer-edged than was the carpenter's adze.

Page 94

Hewing hatchets followed the shape of hewing axes, but, as indicated on the illustrations, they were of smaller dimensions. They were one-handed, their helves were shorter, and though generally bent to the outer side, some were fitted with a handle in the same axis as the eye. They were used for shaping and smoothing smaller timber, the beams and rafters of houses, the ribs of vessels, etc.

The Lathing Hatchet was shaped with a flat top so as to clear the ceiling when driving the nails of the upper laths of partitions and the inside of walls.

The interesting hatchet of Augustus Jones, the early surveyor of Upper Canada, was salvaged many years ago by Levi C. Green, one of the Stoney Creek Greens, to which family Scout

Billy Green of 1813 fame belonged. It was formerly in the collection of the now defunct Stoney Creek Historical Society. It weighs about two pounds. It was used probably in cutting obstructing brush-wood and saplings, shaping boundary posts, and blazing trees when Jones was surveying road allowances and lining out lots.

Page 99

In March, 1803, the ship *Boston*, of Boston, Massachusetts, arrived in Nootka Sound, on the west coast of Vancouver Island, to trade with the Indians. A dispute arose between the captain and Maquina, the Nootka chief. The Indians captured the ship and massacred all the crew, with the exception of John Jewitt, the blacksmith, and Thompson, the sail maker. Their lives were spared, Jewitt's because he was the armourer and able to forge and repair weapons and tools, and Thompson's whom Jewitt pretended was his father. They were held in captivity for three years, when they were rescued by the captain of another ship from Boston. Jewitt settled in New England, and some years later wrote an account of his adventures, which contains much useful and interesting information concerning Indian life on the west coast.

Among primitive races metal articles and workers in metal were always desirable acquisitions. Consequently the lives of smiths and armourers were generally spared to become slaves, and the whites who wished to gain the friendship of Indian tribes often sent gunsmiths to live among them. This practice was followed by the French in seeking the alliance of the Senecas along the Niagara, and later by the English, when many of the employees, interpreters and agents of the Indian Department were also skilled workers in metal.

The illustration shows Maquina watching his captive black-smith at work. The Indian chief wears a dress made of gaudy European trade cloth, sewn together and decorated with brass buttons by Thompson, who, as a sail maker, was able to fashion such materials to suit the native taste.

Page 100

The plan of the fort is taken from a survey made by Col. Nicolls of the Royal Engineers. The fort was reconstructed in 1932-1934 in conformity with this plan of 1816.

The view of the barracks is from a drawing by Lieut. Sempronius Stretton, now in the Public Archives of Canada. Note soldiers chopping out stump, and sawing planks in pit on the bank; also Indian in canoe spearing fish.

Page 103

The first raft on the Ottawa River was conducted by Philemon Wright, from Hull (of which he was the founder), to Montreal, in 1806. The timbers were fastened together with wooden pins and bound with flexible willow withes. The raft was guided by long heavy sweeps on all sides, those in front being used to assist in swinging the raft around to avoid rocks and shallow water.

Page 104

The Conestoga wagon was so called after the Conestoga Valley in Lancaster County, Pennsylvania, where this type of vehicle was developed. Wagons such as this, though generally larger, and drawn by four or six horses, carried most of the freight to the American west, before the railroad came, over the Alleghany Mountains by the great National Highway to Pittsburg and beyond. While the wagon here shown is probably the only specimen of its kind in Canada, the farm wagons generally in use during the period most likely were constructed on similar lines. Many of the settlers of Waterloo County came from this region of Pennsylvania, and were members of pacifist sects, Mennonists, Tunkers, etc., who had migrated from Germany earlier in the eighteenth century.

Page 106

These illustrations show the clothing worn in Lower Canada a century and a half ago. For walking on the slippery streets of Quebec cloth shoes, or stockings worn over ordinary shoes, were worn. Crampons, removable soles with iron spikes, attached to shoes were also worn. Thompson, the building superintendent, complains of the damage done to the handsome new floors of the Chateau Haldimand, at its opening on the Queen's birthday, 18th January, 1787, by the crampons of visitors, which should have been taken off and left at the door. Mrs. Simcoe's Diary mentions that the troops practised walking

131

on snow-shoes on the Plains of Abraham. She also says that women wear hoods lined with eider-down over a muslin cap, as shown in Lambert's drawing. The priest wears a small wig, which was permitted in cold weather.

Page 111

In the earliest years of British rule the merchants of Montreal began to engage in the fur trade and to equip expeditions to the north and west. The route usually followed was by the Ottawa River and the upper great lakes to Grand Portage, near the head of Lake Superior. After 1796, when this neighbourhood was included in the territory of the United States, Fort William, some miles to the east, became the meeting place of the canoes from Montreal and the fur-traders of the north-west interior. Here the trading goods were unloaded, and the packs of the season's furs taken on board the Montreal canoes for their return voyage.

These Montreal canoes were about 36 feet long and 6 feet wide at the middle, and carried from 3 to 4 tons. They were paddled by crews of 8 to 10 voyageurs, who were commonly called "Mangeurs du Lard," or "Pork Eaters," their provisions generally consisting of salt pork and hulled corn or peas. They travelled in "brigades," usually of 4 canoes, to facilitate the passage over the numerous portages on the route. These large canoes were pushed up the steepest places, cushioned on ever-green boughs, or were carried by 6 men, bottom side *up*. They left Lachine in May, reaching the meeting place early in July. The trading goods consisted of coarse woollen cloths, blankets, ammunition, twist and carrot tobacco, thread, lines, twine, hard-ware, cutlery, brass, copper, and iron kettles, silk and cotton handkerchiefs, shoes, nets and fish hooks, spirituous liquors, colours, vermilion especially, beads, silver ornaments, etc.

Meanwhile, the furs gathered in the far north and west were being carried by toboggans and canoes, so as to reach the Lake Superior meeting place by the time of the arrival of the goods from Montreal. For a month or more the portage over the height of land separating the great lakes waterways from those of the northern interior was a busy place, as lines of men laden with packs of furs, or barrels, sacks and bundles of trading goods hurried along the trail to the waiting canoes.

132

The northern canoes were about half the size of those from Montreal: about 25 feet long by 4 feet wide, with a crew of 4 to 6 men. In portaging they were carried by 2 men at bow and 2 at stern, bottom side *down*.

In addition to these, there were also light express canoes, used for the speedy transportation of correspondence, news, and passengers, such as officials and partners of the trading companies. These carried no freight beyond the provisions and baggage of the crew and passengers. They were paddled by a crew of 15 men, specially picked and paid extra wages for a speedy voyage. Dr. Bigsby says that the passengers sat on their rolled-up beds amidships, while the crew squatted in two rows on their bags of provisions, paddling 50 strokes to the minute to voyageur songs so timed, and stopping occasionally for a short spell to rest and smoke.

Much information and numerous pictures are to be found in various numbers of *The Beaver*, the Hudson's Bay Company's quarterly. Schoolcrafts' *Indian Tribes* gives details of the Indian methods of canoe building, and there are scattered references in J. J. Bigsby's *The Shoe and Canoe*, and in the numerous volumes of the Champlain Society publications dealing with the fur-trade and northern exploration.

Page 114

The present Government House is the third building erected for that purpose in Halifax. Its story is told in two brochures published by the Archives of Nova Scotia: *Government House*, and *The Romance of Government House*, by J. S. Martell, under direction of the Archivist, Dr. D. C. Harvey. Its two predecessors had been situated on the property now occupied by the Legislative Building, or "Province House"; the first a temporary structure put up at the time of the settlement in 1749, the second during Lawrence's governorship, of which a view taken by Richard Short is herein shown. Both of these were wooden buildings.

In 1793 Governor Wentworth complained to the Legislature that the house was so badly decayed that it was "in Danger of falling into the Cellar." A considerable sum had recently been spent on repairs and further expenditures were made during the following years; but Wentworth continued his complaints and urged the building of a new Government House which would be worthy of the King's representative. Strongly supported by the Provincial Treasurer, Michael Wallace, he won over the Assembly to the project. A site in the southern suburbs was secured and in September, 1800, the corner stone was laid. Five years later Wentworth moved into the new Government House, unfinished though its rooms were.

Throughout the years of its construction protests were made by the Assembly that it was on a scale far beyond the circumstances of the province, then with a population of but little more than 60,000. By the time that Wentworth retired in 1808 the building had cost more than twice the sum originally authorized: later additions, repairs and furnishings raised the total expenditure to over £31,000.

Among the articles enumerated as having been purchased is a marble chimney piece carved with statuary and ornaments, for which the celebrated British sculptor, Richard Westmacott, in 1804, received the sum of £31-10. Other items contained in a report of 1811 are: For Levee Room: 7 Turkish Sophas, 12 cane bottom Chairs with cushions and covers, 3 Lustres to suspend from ceiling, Looking Glass, Fire Irons and Fenders. For Saloon: A Brussels Carpet, A Fire Rug to match, Fire Screens, Chimney Candlesticks, Mahogany Tables, Chandelier, Looking Glasses, A Steel Register Stove. For Dining Room: 24 Mahogany Chairs, Floor Cloth for Mahogany Sideboard, Curtains, Draperies, Set of Mahogany Dining Tables. Grates in 2 Waiting Rooms. 2 Lanthorns and 2 Footscrapers in Hall. Smoke Jack and Stone Plate in Kitchen. Brass Register Stove in Nursery.

Page 115

Stoves of some kind were in use in Canada much earlier than is commonly supposed. There is mention of them during the French period. Mrs. Simcoe, in her Diary, says that grates were tried for heating the "canvas house" in which they lived at Newark, but these not answering, stoves were substituted; she also mentions their use in Quebec, and complains of the overheating of the houses in winter.

At the St. Maurice Forges in Lower Canada, stoves were manufactured during the eighteenth century, their characteristic product, known as the Three River Stove, was the "two-decker" box stove, with fire box below and oven above. Stoves long enough to hold a cord-wood stick were sometimes used to heat two rooms by placing it midway of an opening cut in the dividing wall.

Benjamin Franklin invented an open stove for heating. In a pamphlet which he published in 1744 he describes his "newly invented Pennsylvania fire places, composed of five iron plates scru'd and fixed together, with one side open." While retaining its original basic construction, the "Franklin" stove was furnished with various fittings, such as brass railings, and was often decorated with castings of illustrations of Biblical stories.

The first iron foundry in Upper Canada was established about 1820 in Norfolk County by Joseph Van Norman and his partners, the ore being procured from extensive bogs in Charlotteville. The principal products of this Normandale Furnace were bar-iron for blacksmiths, axes, and stoves. The foundry carried on an extensive and profitable business for several years, but about 1852 it ceased to exist owing to financial losses, and the depletion of bog-ore in the immediate vicinity. In 1829 the foundry was placed under the management of Elijah Leonard, an experienced American iron-worker, who later founded the firm of E. Leonard and Sons, in London, Ont., and became a Dominion Senator. In a published autobiography of the family the furnace is described as consisting of a brick stack or chimney about thirty feet high built on the side of a hill. "Motive power was obtained from a stream which turned an overshot wheel about fourteen feet in diameter that drove a double piston bellows by means of cranks. Only one tuyère (pipe through which air is forced) was employed to admit the blast. The ore and charcoal were mixed in the top house, being dumped into the furnace by barrows, and the iron when melted ran down into a hearth about two feet wide and five feet long. Into this receptacle we dipped our ladles and carried off the product direct to the flasks. When in full blast we took off two heats in twenty-four hours." The site can still be seen, but no vestige of the buildings remains. The information about the Normandale Furnace is taken from *Pioneer Sketches of the Long Point Settlement*, by E. A. Owen.

All able-bodied men were enrolled in the Canadian militia. They received occasional training in drill during the year, but the principal muster was on the birthday of King George III, June 4th. Many of them were without fire-arms, and carried sticks, pitchforks, pikes and umbrellas as substitutes. Only a few, veterans of the Revolutionary War or disbanded soldiers, had uniforms. Two of these are shown in the illustration on the left; one of them, a sergeant, is dressing the line with his halbert held horizontally. It is stated that in the battle of Queenston in 1812 none of the militia wore uniforms.

PART THREE

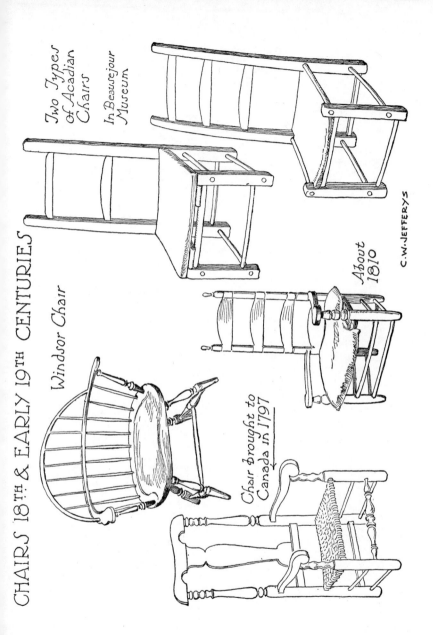

CHAIRS 18TH & EARLY 19TH CENTURIES

Two Types of Acadian Chairs

In Beausejour Museum

Windsor Chair

About 1810

Chair brought to Canada in 1797

C.W.JEFFERYS

SEVEN MORE CHAIRS

French Canadian Chairs
Note backward slant of Acadian & French Canadian chairs. Latter in Chateau de Ramezay

In → Fort Anne Museum

Acadian Chair

British Canadian & American types. Seats often made of splints or rushes →

Early Rocking Chairs

C. W. JEFFERYS

140

INDIANS BREAKING INTO A BEAVER HOUSE

C.W.JEFFERYS

ROMAN CATHOLIC BISHOPS

MGR J.O.Briand 1766-84

MGR J.O.Plessis 1801-25

Rabat

Roman Collar

MGR J.J.Lartigue 1836-49

MGR Ignace Bourget 1840-76

METHODIST MINISTERS

Elder
William
Case

Dr.
Nathan
Bangs

Rev.
William
Black
N.S.

Bishop
James
Richardson

Rev
William
Ryerson

Rev
James
Evans

143

TYPICAL WOMEN of the TIME:

Lady Wentworth
From Painting by
J.S. Copley R.A.

Lady MacNab
From daguerrotype

Reproduced in
Morgan's "Types of
Canadian Women"
Daughters of
Hon. W. McGillivray

M.me de
St. Laurent

Lady
Hunter

MORE TYPICAL WOMEN

Lady Johnson

Mrs John Scadding
Jr

Lady
Dorchester

Lady
Sarah
Maitland

Mrs.
William
Allan

Mme.
Joly

Courtesy of
Dr Crawford
Scadding

Mrs John
Scadding
Jr

Mme.
Joseph
Papineau

DAVID THOMPSON TAKING AN OBSERVATION

DAVID THOMPSON IN THE ATHABASCA PASS, 1810

NOTRE DAME
MONTREAL

Place d'Armes
From drawing by
R. Dillon
c. 1808

*The Old Church
and the New*
1829

*From painting by
Georges Delfosse*

QUEBEC CHURCH FURNISHINGS

Sanctuary Lamp

Altar with Badalquin
St. François de Sales
Pointe~aux~Trembles
Portneuf

Holy Water
Bowl

Easter
Candlestick

C.W. JEFFERYS

INTERIOR FEATURES
of QUEBEC
CHURCHES

Pulpit in Church at Les
Eboulements

Churchwardens' Pew
St. Pierre Ile d'Orleans

A Typical Altar
St. Pierre, I.O. from drawing
by R.C.Betts

SHRINES
by the
ROADSIDE

Chapel
Ile d'Orleans

Wayside
Chapel
L'Ange Gardien

Near
Lorette

On
Côté de Beaupré

C.W. JEFFERYS

151

PROTESTANT CHURCHES in QUEBEC

Church of England, Chambly.

J.W. JEFFERYS.

Tower of Church of England Three Rivers

Cuthbert Family Chapel, Berthier-en-haut.

BLOCK HOUSES

Diagonal Blockhouse ↓

At Fort York, Toronto

At Kingston Mills to guard Rideau Canal

Stone Blockhouse in Fort Wellington, Prescott, Ont.

Shingle-covered Blockhouse in Fort Edward, Windsor, N.S.

153

MARTELLO TOWERS

C.W. JEFFERYS

On Plains of ↑
Abraham,
Quebec →

Two of four Towers
extending from
St Lawrence to
St Charles Valley.
Built 1805-1823

Named incorrectly
after Cape Mort-
ella, Corsica where
a few French troops in a tower, with 3 small guns, res-
isted for some time attack
by British warships in 1794

Temporary
Roof →

Similar towers
at Saint John, N.B.
& Kingston
Ont

At Point Pleasant, Halifax

154

MEETING OF BROCK AND TECUMSEH, 1812

BROCK'S RIDE TO QUEENSTON, 1812

PORTRAITS and RELICS of GENERAL BROCK

Coat worn by Brock at
Queenston, showing hole
made by fatal bullet.
In Archives of Canada, Ottawa.

Miniature   painted by
J. Hudson in   England on
Brock's last visit in 1806.

Brock's Hat.
In Museum, Niagara-on-the-Lake.

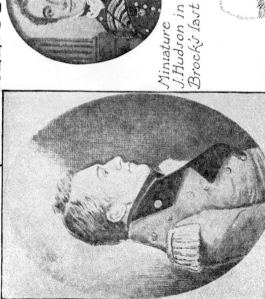

Drawing in Water-colour &
Chalk, dated 1811. Artist unknown.
In possession of relatives, Guernsey.

BRITISH UNIFORMS WAR of 1812

Private

General

←White
←Red

Belts, Lace
& Buttons
White

Grey →

Captain

←White
←Red

Buttons
&
Lace
Gold

White →

Sergeant

←Red
←White

All Coats
Scarlet

White
↓

Sashes
Crimson

Grey Trousers

C.W.J.

UNIFORMS of the WAR of 1812.

Grenadiers
8th, Kings,
Regiment.

Scarlet
Coat,
Blue Facings,
Dark Grey
Trousers,
Waterproof
Cap worn
over Shako
in Stormy
weather

Trooper
19th Light
Dragoons
Blue, Facings Yellow.

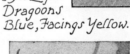

Officer,
Light Infantry
Company,
41st Regt.
Scarlet Coat.
Green Feather
on Shako.
Gilt Chain Fringe
on shoulders.
Grey Trousers.
Curved Sabre.

Captain, U.S.Infantry, 1813.

FORTS at the MOUTH of the NIAGARA

Ft. Niagara   Ft. George   Newark   Lighthouse   Battery

Entrance to Niagara River. From drawing made in 1815, before the capture of Fort George. Published in the Port Folio, July, 1817.

Fort Niagara from Fort George. Drawing by B.J. Lossing in his Pictorial Field Book of the War of 1812.

Powder Magazine Ft. George. Built 1796.

BATTLE OF STONEY CREEK, 1813

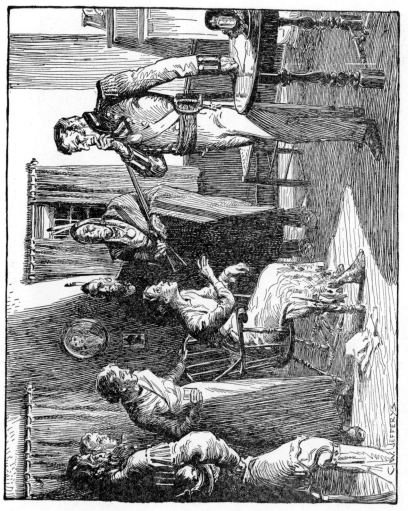

LAURA SECORD TELLS HER STORY TO FITZGIBBON 1813

BEAVER DAMS & BURLINGTON HEIGHTS

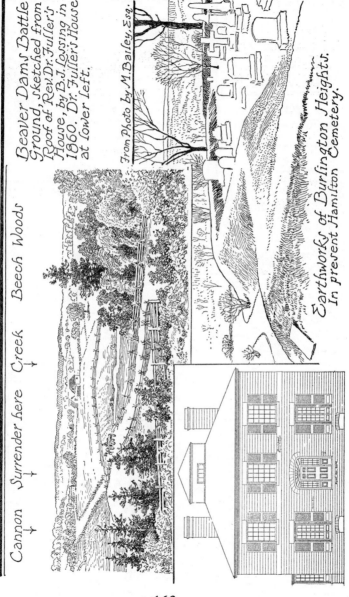

Beaver Dams Battle Ground, sketched from Roof of Rev. Dr. Fuller's House, by B.J. Lossing in 1860. Dr. Fuller's House at lower left.

From Photo by M. Bailey, Esq.

Cannon   Surrender here   Creek   Beech Woods

Earthworks of Burlington Heights. In present Hamilton Cemetery.

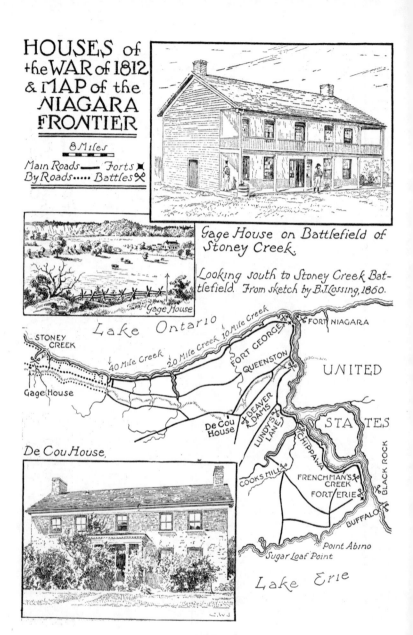

HOUSES of the WAR of 1812 & MAP of the NIAGARA FRONTIER

8 Miles

Main Roads —— Forts ✕
By Roads ····· Battles ✕

Gage House on Battlefield of Stoney Creek.

Looking south to Stoney Creek Battlefield. From sketch by B.J.Lossing, 1860.

Gage House

Lake Ontario

STONEY CREEK

40 Mile Creek   20 Mile Creek   10 Mile Creek

FORT NIAGARA

FORT GEORGE

QUEENSTON

UNITED

Gage House

De Cou House

BEAVER DAMS

LUNDY'S LANE

STATES

De Cou House.

COOKS MILL

CHIPPAWA

FRENCHMAN'S CREEK

FORT ERIE

BLACK ROCK

BUFFALO

Point Abino

Sugar Loaf Point

Lake Erie

The MARCH of the 104th

Route of Regiment ......

RIVIÈRE DU LOUP
MALBAIE
St. ANDRÉ
LAKE TEMISCOUATA
BAIE St. PAUL
RIVIÈRE-OUELLE
MADAWASKA R
To KINGSTON
QUEBEC
MONTMAGNY
St. LAWRENCE
St. JOHN R.
St. Leonard
GRAND FALLS
QUEBEC
MAINE
NEW BRUNSWICK
RIVER
Woodstock
St. JOHN
FREDERICTON
Ste. CROIX R.
SAINT JOHN

General Sir Martin Hunter.
From photograph in N.B. Museum
of miniature in possession of Major
A.G. Bates at Coldstream, Scotland.
Courtesy of G.H. Markham, Esq.
Saint John, N.B.

Captain Charles Rainsford
on his way to Rivière du Loup
to get supplies for the Regiment. From photo of drawing formerly in
possession of Moodie Rainsford, Esq. Grand Falls, N.B. Courtesy G.H. Markham.

TECUMSEH AT THE BATTLE OF THE THAMES, 1813

C.W.JEFFERYS

THE *SHANNON* AND THE *CHESAPEAKE* ENTERING HALIFAX HARBOUR, 1813

From lithograph by L. Haghe of painting by J. C. Schetzke, designed by Capt. R. H. King, R.N.

ARTILLERY

Monogram & Crown
of George III on
24 Pounder

← Wood

Iron

24 Pound Cannon

Wood →

← Iron

Short Range Ship Carronade

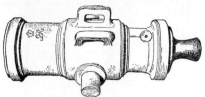

Bronze Field Cannon

Light
Field
Gun

Wood

Bronze Howitzer

6 Pounder Field Gun

Sir James
Yeo
Portrait by
A.Buck.

Sir Gordon Drummond
Portrait by Berthon
in J.Ross Robertson Collection
Toronto Public Library

Silhouette
of
Lt.-Col.
John
Macdonell
In possession of
J.A.Macdonell K.C.
Alexandria.

Sir George Prevost
Painting in Archives of Canada.

Captain
Robert
Barclay

Lieut - Col. Charles
de Salaberry
Lithograph from portrait by
A.Dickinson, in Archives
of Canada.

Lt. Col.
John
Harvey

171

AMERICAN COMMANDERS : WAR of 1812

Gen.
Jacob
Brown

From
Portrait by
J.W.Jarvis
City Hall New York

Commodore
Isaac Chauncey

Painting in City Hall
New York

Gen.
Winfield Scott
From Engraving.
after Wood, in
Analectic
Magazine
1814

Gen.James
Wilkinson

From Portrait by
C.W.Peale in Indepen-
dence Hall, Philadelphia.

Gen.William
Henry
Harrison
From
Engraving
after
Wood, in
Analectic
Magazine

From
Portrait by
Jarvis, in
City Hall New York.

Captain
Oliver Hazard
Perry

DE SALABERRY AT CHATEAUGUAY, 1813

C.W. JEFFERYS

BATTLE OF LUNDY'S LANE, 1814

From painting in water colour by C. W. Jefferys, in City Hall Toronto.

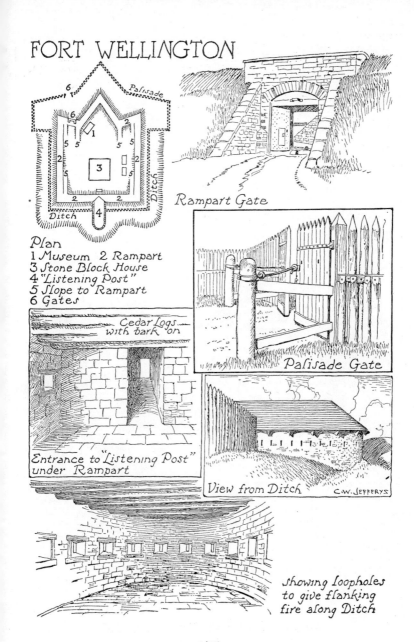

FORT WELLINGTON

6   Palisade

Plan
1 Museum 2 Rampart
3 Stone Block House
4 "Listening Post"
5 Slope to Rampart
6 Gates

Ditch
Ditch

Rampart Gate

Cedar Logs with bark on

Palisade Gate

Entrance to "Listening Post" under Rampart

View from Ditch

C.W. JEFFERYS

showing loopholes
to give flanking
fire along Ditch

MÉTIS HUNTING THE BUFFALO

THE RED RIVER CART

C.W. JEFFERYS

No iron was used. The frame was held together with wooden pegs. The tires were bound round with strips of "Shaganhappi", raw fresh skin of buffalo or cattle, which as it dried, shrank & held them tightly, forming a hard & durable rim. These carts followed the Métis hunting parties & carried the meat of the slain buffalo. They were also employed in transporting freight. Sometimes they were fitted with a round-topped hood of hide or canvas.

THE FIGHT AT SEVEN OAKS 1816

LORD SELKIRK NAMING KILDONAN, 1817

EARLY VIEWS of RED RIVER

Interior of Settler's House.
This picture and that of
Fort Gibraltar probably were
drawn by Peter Rindisbacher.
Originals in Public Archives
of Canada, Ottawa

Fort Gibraltar,
from Assiniboine
River, 1821.

180

WINTER TRAVEL IN THE WEST

Dog Cariole at the Hudson's Bay 1825.

The Governor of Red River driving his Family in a Horse Cariole.

From Coloured Lithographs by W. Day, in Archives of Canada.

Backhouse Mill, near Port Rowan, Norfolk County, Ont. Built 1808.

Note Overshot Wheel & Flume for Mill Race

C.W. JEFFERYS

182

A GRIST MILL

183

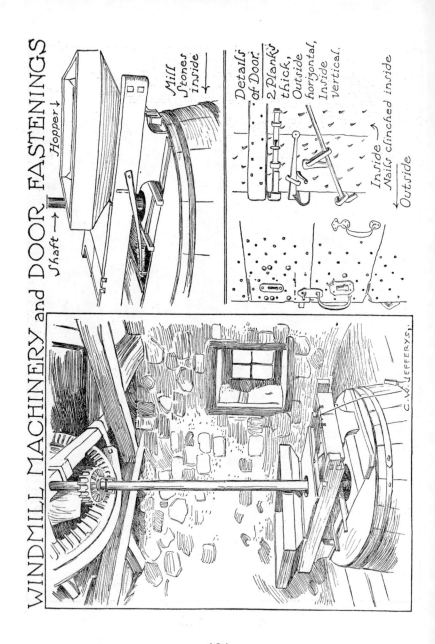

WINDMILL MACHINERY and DOOR FASTENINGS

Shaft →

Hopper ↓

Mill Stones inside ↓

Details of Door.

2 Planks thick, Outside horizontal, Inside vertical.

Inside ↗
Nails clinched inside
Outside ↘

C. W. JEFFERYS.

MILL DAM
and SAW
MILL.

From "Sketches in New
Brunswick."
Lithographs by S. Russell,
after sketches by P. Harry,
W. P. Kay & E. N. Kendall, R.N.

Courtesy of
W. H. Coverdale, Esq.

Building the Mill Dam.
Pine & elm logs placed in direction of stream, crossed by others notched into them, crosswise,
the whole loaded with stones.
On left is birch timber frame
of Flume for water to Mill Wheel.

In Manoir Richelieu Collection.

COLONEL THOMAS TALBOT

FORTE ET FIDELE

Born Ireland 1771. Secretary to Lt. Gov. Simcoe 1792-4. Settled on Lake Erie 1801 & colonized district. Died London U.C. 1853. Buried Tyrconnel Ont.

Chair used by Colonel Talbot. In Library of University of Western Ontario, London

From Water Colour Portrait by J.D. Wandesforde. In Library, University of Western Ontario, London, Ont.

Sketch of Talbot's Residence Port Talbot
From "The Diary of Mrs. Simcoe."

186

NOTES ON PART THREE

Page 141

Before the introduction of steel traps, the Indians caught the beaver by piercing a hole in the roof of the house with an ice-chisel, set into a heavy six-foot pole, after barring the underwater outlet with stakes driven through the ice. Observe the open water in the middle of the pond to the right, and below the dam to the right, the distant beaver houses already broken open, and the dog, whose instinct enables him to detect the presence of the beaver in the house. David Thompson's *Narrative* describes the method of hunting in detail.

Page 142

The Catholic clergy in Canada, during the French regime and until about 1860-1875, wore a sort of tab beneath the chin, called a "Rabat." This was a piece of black cloth or silk, divided into two oblong parts, edged with white. Such had been the custom in France and Belgium, from whence came the early priests serving in Canada, and naturally the same practice was followed in this country. In time it came to be associated particularly with those who supported the principles of the national church of France, which claimed certain rights independent of the jurisdiction of the Pope. These were known as Gallicans, while in opposition to them were the Ultramontanes, those who believed that all ecclesiastical power was concentrated in the Roman Pontiff. About the middle of the nineteenth century, a movement in favour of Ultramontane principles had made considerable progress, which led toward greater conformity to Roman customs, even in such minor matters as dress. Bishop Bourget, of Montreal, after a visit to Europe, issued a letter to his clergy in 1861, urging them to discard the "Rabat" and adopt the "Roman Collar." Other bishops followed his action, and the change became general, though some, especially in the diocese of Quebec, regarded as the stronghold of Gallicanism, continued to wear the Rabat until 1875, when Mgr. E. A. Taschereau ordered the substitution of the Roman Collar.

Page 143

William Black, 1760-1834, "the father of Methodism in Nova Scotia," was born in Yorkshire, and came to Nova Scotia with his parents in 1775. He became a preacher in 1780 and eventually was appointed General Superintendent of Wesleyan Missions in British America.

William Case, 1780-1855, was born in Massachusetts. He was first stationed on the Bay of Quinte. Later he became Presiding Elder of the Methodist Church in Canada and the United States, and Superintendent of the Wesleyan Methodist Church in Canada. In 1828 he was Superintendent of Indian Missions in Upper Canada, and from 1837 to 1851 in charge of the Wesleyan Indian School at Alnwick, Ontario, where he died.

Nathan Bangs came to Canada as a teacher and surveyor. Converted to Methodism, he was sent to organize a circuit in the Long Point settlement on Lake Erie. Here and in the Niagara district, on Yonge Street, on the Bay of Quinte, on the Thames, at Detroit and Quebec, he laboured until 1807, when he was transferred to the United States. He visited Canada frequently thereafter.

James Richardson, 1795-1875, born in Kingston, served in the Provincial Marine, and lost an arm at Sackett's Harbour in 1813. He joined the Methodist Episcopal Church in 1818, became a local preacher, and an itinerant minister in 1824. He was editor of *The Christian Guardian* in 1832. Bishop of the Methodist Episcopal Church of Canada in 1858.

James Evans, 1801-1846, born in England, came to Canada in 1823. Was teacher at the Indian school at Rice Lake in 1828. Ordained minister in 1833, he was sent as missionary to the St. Clair Indians in 1834, to Lake Superior in 1834, and thence to the Indians of the North-West, where he was stationed at Norway House.

Five sons of Col. Joseph Ryerson, of Long Point, became Methodist ministers, George, William, John, Edwy and Egerton, the most noted.

For information on the early Methodist ministers consult *Case and his Cotemporaries*, by Rev. John Carroll, Playter's *History of Methodism in Canada*, and *The First Century of Methodism in Canada*, by Rev. J. E. Sanderson. The latter contains many portraits.

Page 144

Frances Deering, born Boston, Mass., married 1769, John Wentworth (later knighted), Governor of New Hampshire, and

Surveyor-General of the King's Woods in North America, two weeks after the death of her first husband. At the Revolution, Wentworth, as a Loyalist, went to England. In 1792 he was appointed Lieutenant-Governor of Nova Scotia. Lady Wentworth is described by contemporary chroniclers as beautiful, accomplished and gay. She died in England in 1813, aged sixty-eight. Her husband survived her until 1820, dying at the age of eighty-four. Their country estate at Bedford Basin was lent to the Duke of Kent, who occupied it with Madame de St. Laurent during his stay at Halifax. Copley's portrait shows the costume of the late eighteenth century.

Mary, eldest daughter of John Stuart, Sheriff of the Johnstown District, Upper Canada, married, 1831, Allan Napier MacNab. She died in 1846, while her husband was Speaker of the Legislative Assembly. He was knighted for his services in the Rebellion of 1837, and became Prime Minister of Canada. The portrait illustrates the fashion of hair dressing and the sleeves and bodice of the late eighteen-forties.

Alphonsine Thérèse Bernardine Julie de Montgenet de St. Laurent, Baronne de Fortisson, met Prince Edward, Duke of Kent, in Martinique. She accompanied him to Quebec, and here and in Nova Scotia and in England, for twenty-eight years she lived with him as his morganatic wife, presiding over his household with dignity and propriety. On the marriage of the Duke to the widow of the Prince of Leiningen in 1818 for reasons of state, she retired to a convent. Both she and the Duke were close friends of the de Salaberry family, and acted as god-parents to one of the younger sons. The portrait is from a miniature of the early nineteenth century.

The two young women were daughters of the Hon. William McGillivray, a member of the Legislative Council of Lower Canada, and a director of the North West Company of fur traders. The portraits show the costume and hair-dressing of about 1820-1830. Note the high waist and straight girdle, in contrast to the deep pointed bodice of the later period worn by Lady MacNab.

Lady Hunter, Jean Dickson, heiress of James Dickson, of Anton's Hill, Berwickshire, married Lieut.-Col. Martin Hunter in 1797, and died in 1844. When her husband was appointed

Brigadier-General in command of the forces in the Maritime Provinces in 1803, she followed him with her children the next year. Letters and journals written by herself and her husband, containing much valuable material on the social conditions of the time, have been privately printed. Transcripts of them are in the possession of Mr. G. H. Markham, of Saint John, N.B., to whom I am indebted for copies of their portraits, and much information concerning them. Her letters reveal her as an acute observer, with a sense of humour and a faculty of graphic description. They are a source of information for the social history of the Maritime Provinces from 1803 to 1812 as valuable as the *Diary of Mrs. Simcoe* is for Upper Canada.

Page 145

These pages have been designed to illustrate not only characteristic women of the time, but also to show styles of hairdressing and costume.

Mary Watts, of a distinguished New York family, married, 1773, Sir John Johnson, son of Sir William Johnson. Her husband succeeded his father as Superintendent-General of Indian Affairs. On the outbreak of the Revolution he escaped to Canada, and his wife was held in New York for some time as a hostage for him. Later she joined him in Montreal, where she died in 1815. The portrait shows her wearing a draped cap in vogue during the latter years of the nineteenth century for house wear.

Melicent Triges (1768-1860), wife of John Scadding, Sr., of York, U.C. The portrait evidently was painted during the eighteen-thirties, as shown by the puffed sleeves, spreading cape and high-waisted girdle. The crimped and beribboned cap, worn indoors by elderly women, is characteristic of the period.

Amelia Playter (1806-1902), wife of John Scadding, Jr., wears the wide out-door hat, the curls, and the spreading lace cape of the eighteen-thirties.

Leah (1790-1848), daughter of Dr. John Gamble, married Hon. William Allan, a leading citizen of York, U.C., who, as Major of Militia, signed the capitulation of the town to the Americans in 1813. Their son was Senator George W. Allan, of Moss Park, the patron of Paul Kane, the painter of Indians. She is shown wearing a lace house cap of the early forties. Note also the smoothly parted hair, as in Lady Maitland's portrait, which followed the elaborate curly coiffure of the preceding two decades, such as is seen in the portrait of

Madame Joly, Julie de Lotbinière (1810-1887), of a distinguished French-Canadian family, who married, 1828, G. P. G. Joly. Of their two sons, the elder became Sir Henri G. Joly, K.C.M.G., and Lieutenant-Governor of British Columbia; the other, Edmond, joined the British Army, and served in the Crimea and the Indian Mutiny where, after many dangerous adventures, he was killed at the relief of Lucknow. Mme. Joly's portrait is evidently of the eighteen-twenties or early thirties, as shown by the curled hair and high-waisted girdle.

Rosalie Chevrier, in 1780, married Joseph Papineau, who distinguished himself as a constitutional leader in the Lower Canadian House of Assembly. She died in the cholera epidemic of 1832 in Montreal, aged seventy-four. She was the mother of the celebrated Louis Joseph Papineau. She wears a mob cap of the early nineteenth century.

Lady Sarah Lennox, daughter of the Duke of Richmond, married, 1815, Sir Peregrine Maitland. It is said that they met at the famous ball given by her mother in Brussels on the eve of Waterloo. Her father having refused his consent to their marriage, they eloped and she became Maitland's wife. Her father soon became reconciled, and when he was appointed Governor of British North America in 1818, Maitland was made Lieutenant-Governor of Upper Canada, and ten years later, of Nova Scotia. After the tragic death of the Duke of Richmond from hydrophobia, Maitland acted as Administrator until the appointment of the Earl of Dalhousie in 1820. Sir Peregrine and Lady Sarah spent much of their time on their country estate at Stamford, U.C. The dress shown in the portrait indicates that it was painted during the forties. Note the India shawl of the pattern familiar in the Paisley shawl.

Romance is also connected with Lady Dorchester, Lady Maria Howard. She and her elder sister, Lady Anne, were daughters of Lord Howard of Effingham. He was an intimate friend of Guy Carleton, later Lord Dorchester, and when he asked the hand of Lady Anne her father gladly gave his consent. But the lady was already in love with Carleton's nephew, and

191

refused Guy's proposal. On returning after the interview to her waiting sister and their bosom friend, Miss Seymour, who were awaiting her, they observed her distressed expression, which she explained by saying that she had "just had to refuse the best man on earth." "The more fool you," remarked her younger sister, then aged eighteen, "I only wish he had given me the chance!" Some time later Miss Seymour confided the story to the rejected suitor. Carleton took the hint, and though more than double the age of Lady Maria, proposed to her, was accepted, married her and lived happily ever after. His nephew married Lady Anne, and later served under his rejected uncle. Lady Dorchester is described as being small, fair, upright, and extremely dignified and ceremonious, in the manner of the French court of Versailles, where she had been brought up.

Page 146

Thompson is using an artificial horizon. This is a flat iron pan into which mercury was poured. The pan is covered by a sloping glass roof, and placed on perfectly level and firm ground or rock in a situation to reflect the image of the sun. The surveyor looks through the eye-piece of his sextant at this reflected image, and finds the angle which gives the elevation of the sun at its meridian above the horizon. From this he is able to calculate his position.

Notice in the illustration the iron bottle in which the mercury is carried, the note-book and pencil, and the camp in the middle distance, far enough from the observer to prevent any disturbance of the surface of the mercury by the tread of horses or men. The length of the shadows and the distance of the artificial horizon from the observer show that the observation is being taken in autumn. For detailed information on early methods of surveying I am indebted to Dr. J. B. Tyrrell, of Toronto.

Page 148

Richard Dillon was the proprietor of a hotel on the south-west corner of St. James Street and the Place d'Armes in Montreal. It was very popular from about 1790 to 1815. Dillon was an amateur artist, and painted panoramas, and several views of Montreal, which have considerable historic value.

The illustration showing the old and new churches (the latter the present existing building) gives an excellent idea of their relative positions. As may be seen, the old church stood in the middle of Notre Dame Street, opposite the Seminary of St. Sulpice, the wall of which is shown on the lower right of the picture.

Georges Delfosse (1869-1939), the painter of this picture and of that of Nelson's Column, was an accomplished French-Canadian artist who depicted a large number of the old streets and buildings of Montreal. His paintings are admirable in composition and suffused with light and colour.

Page 152

Most of the early Protestant churches in Lower Canada were built in the same style as the Catholic churches of the period: the classical or late Renaissance, with some trace of the influence of Wren and Gibbs, the English architects, whose work was inspired by the same ideals. The Protestant churches, however, were not built with the semi-circular apse or chancel, nor did they possess the side chapels, both characteristic features of the Catholic churches, and were simpler in plan and in their interior furnishings.

The Church of England and its rectory at Three Rivers were originally the Church and Presbytère of the Recollets, built during the French regime.

The Cuthbert family chapel is built of stone, covered with rough-cast. It was restored some years ago under the direction of Roy Wilson, A.R.C.A., architect.

Page 159

British regiments or battalions consisted normally of ten companies, two of which were composed of specially selected men: a Light Infantry company, of active, alert men, generally good marksmen, employed as skirmishers, and a Grenadier company of the largest and heaviest men, who led in bayonet charges and close fighting. When the regiment was drawn up in line, the Grenadier company was stationed on the right and the Light Infantry company on the left.

By law all able-bodied men between the ages of sixteen and sixty, with the exception of those belonging to pacifist sects, such as Quakers and Mennonists, were obliged to serve in the Canadian Militia. This force was known as the "Sedentary" Militia. From it was obtained for active service the "Embodied"

Militia, composed of volunteers and those chosen by ballot. Two companies, known as flank companies, were drawn from the battalions of Embodied Militia, each consisting of one hundred picked men under the age of forty, who were drilled six days a month, and could be called out at a moment's notice, and kept on active duty as long as their service was necessary. During the War of 1812 they were often called out to meet invasion, and there is frequent mention of their being released for a time to go home to sow or reap their crops, many of them being farmers.

In addition to the Militia, battalions of Canadian Regulars, such as the Glengarry Light Infantry, the Fencibles, Voltigeurs, the Newfoundland Regiment, etc., enlisted for the duration of the war.

The American forces in the War of 1812 consisted of the Regular Army, the United States Volunteers, enlisted for shorter terms of service both under Federal authority, and the Militia of the different States of the Union, enlisted also for short terms and not obliged to serve outside of their respective States without State authority.

The John Ross Robertson Collection in the Toronto Public Library contains many coloured drawings showing uniforms of British regiments which had served in Canada. These are most useful; but the student must be warned that in some cases the uniforms depicted, while those of the regiment and correct as to facings, etc., are not such as were worn *at the time* they were stationed in Canada. In particular it should be noted that by 1812 pigtailed hair and knee breeches had been discarded. The hair was cut to conform to the shape of the head, long trousers, slightly split at the ankles, were substituted for breeches, and stiff shakos had taken the places of the earlier broadside cocked hats.

Pages 160 and 163

The pictures of the battlefields of Beaver Dams and Stoney Creek, and of the forts at the mouth of the Niagara are from sketches by Benson J. Lossing, author and illustrator of *The Field Book of the War of 1812*, which contains woodcuts of these and many other historic places, showing their appearance at the time they were made, about 1869.

Page 164

The Gage house, on the battlefield of Stoney Creek, is still standing, though its western portion, used as a store, was torn down about 1896. It is furnished and kept in excellent repair by its owners, the Wentworth Women's Historical Society, and contains many pieces of old furniture, pictures and other relics.

The De Cou house, Fitz Gibbon's headquarters, and the objective of Laura Secord's journey in 1813, is now owned by the Ontario Hydro-Electric Commission, which has carefully preserved it and its surroundings. The interior was damaged by fire shortly before its acquisition, but its walls are intact, and the building will be restored and made a historic shrine.

Page 165

The 104th Regiment was formed in 1810 out of the New Brunswick Fencibles, raised in 1803, and was incorporated in the British regular Army. It was recruited mainly in New Brunswick, and partly in Nova Scotia, and included also a number of Canadians from Quebec; and was composed of hardy woodsmen and hunters, accustomed to the use of the snowshoe, the canoe, the axe and the musket.

The march of the regiment from Fredericton, N.B., to Kingston, U.C., in 1813, was one of the most famous in the history of the British Army. On Feb. 16th the Grenadier Company started from Fredericton, followed on each succeeding day by a Battalion Company, the rearguard, the Light Infantry Company, leaving on the 21st. The six companies, 550 rank and file, reached Quebec on March 19th, with the loss of only one man. Thence it proceeded to Kingston, where it arrived in the middle of April, and by the summer of 1813 was in action on the Niagara frontier, and took part next year in the battles of Chippewa and Lundy's Lane.

The first few days of the march were through settled country and over beaten roads. Thereafter their way led through the forest. Each man and officer took turn in breaking the trail. Every fifteen minutes the leading man stepped aside, until the whole company had passed him, when he threw off his snowshoes and marched in the rear on the hard beaten path. Knapsacks, arms, bedding and provisions were carried on toboggans, the line of the company in single file being nearly half a mile long. At night they camped in rough huts of evergreen branches covered with brush. The weather was unusually cold, and the snow the deepest in ten years.

At the south end of Lake Temisconata, two companies became stormbound and food ran short. Captain Charles Rainsford and two French-Canadian privates made a forced march to Riviere-du-Loup for relief, returning with provisions after a journey of ninety miles in two days and two nights.

Sir Martin Hunter (1757-1846), who raised the regiment and was its first colonel, was born in Durham County, England. He entered the army, and served in the Revolutionary War till 1778, fighting as ensign in the battle of Bunker's Hill. Later he saw service in India, the Mediterranean and the West Indies. In 1803 he was appointed Brigadier-General in North America, and commanded the troops in the Maritime Provinces. For a time he acted as Lieutenant-Governor of New Brunswick. He was recalled to England in 1812, and knighted in 1832.

I am indebted to Mr. G. H. Markham, of Saint John, N.B., for information on the 104th, gathered from letters of Captains Le Couteux and Playfair, and on Sir Martin and Lady Hunter, and also for their portraits, from their Journal and Letters privately printed.

Page 166

It is said that in the battle of Lake Erie, owing to insufficient and defective fuses, the cannon of Barclay's fleet had to be fired by discharging pistols into their touch-holes. Notice the officer shouting his commands through a speaking trumpet, and the boy in the left foreground carrying a pail of powder (and commonly called a "powder-monkey"), with thumb against his ear, to deaden the concussion caused by gun fire. It was the custom of artillerymen to thrust their thumbs into their ears, and to rise on their toes when their guns were fired. Mrs. Simcoe in her *Diary* relates that Lieutenant-Governor Simcoe suffered long and severe head pain from the discharge of a cannon from the rampart of Fort Niagara, beneath which he was standing.

Page 170

Artillery in Canada during the period covered by this volume consisted of two kinds: stationary cannon, generally of large calibre, used for the defense or siege of forts, and on board warships, and lighter weight field cannon accompanying infantry in fighting in the open. Heavy cannon threw solid iron balls weighing from eighteen to thirty-six pounds; field guns ranged generally from three pounders to eight pounders. In addition to these were mortars and howitzers, short thick cannon, resting on the ground or low carriages, with their muzzles elevated to give a plunging fire, both using exploding shells. The largest guns were of iron, many of the smaller ones, as well as howitzers, were of brass.

Field guns and ammunition wagons were drawn by horses; in the War of 1812 horses and their drivers formed what was known as the Car Brigade; the horses were hired or requisitioned from the farms, their drivers were hired or impressed civilians. These were sometimes Quakers, Mennonites, or other conscientious objectors to warfare, who were pressed into the service of transporting ammunition and supplies.

Transportation of the heavy guns up the waterways was a slow, difficult and expensive undertaking. Oxen were employed in places to haul the boats where the current was too strong for poling. Warships on the lakes were armed with cannon of various calibres, from thirty-two pounders to some as small as two and three pounders. The big guns were of two kinds: long range guns, and carronades. The latter were short thick cannon (so named from the place where they originally were made, Carron Iron Works in Scotland), with a large bore, firing a heavy charge of small projectiles. They did tremendous execution in close action, but were inferior to long guns at a distance of about a quarter of a mile. On Lake Ontario the British fleet had more carronades than long guns, consequently it sought to bring the enemy to close quarters, while the Americans manœuvred so as to fight at a distance where their more numerous long guns would give them an advantage. At Plattsburg in 1814, however, these conditions were reversed, and to this and the enclosed space in which the battle was fought, the Americans, to a large degree, owed their success.

In all these guns several kinds of projectiles were used, grape shot, shells, and solid round balls. The latter sometimes were heated red hot, so as to set on fire whatever inflammable objects they struck. In the American Fort Niagara today may be seen one of the furnaces used for heating shot. Grape shot were used to scatter bullets among masses of troops.

These cannon were all muzzle loaders, fired by inserting a lighted fuse, held by a linstock, a long pole, in a touch-hole near the base of the cannon. When a cannon had to be abandoned it was often rendered useless for a while by "spiking" it, i.e. driving an iron rod or a steel bayonet tightly into the touch-hole. The gun then could not be used until the spike had been drilled out.

Page 171 and 172

For data on British and American commanders in the War of 1812, see *The War with the United States*, by William Wood, in the Chronicles of Canada Series, and *Select Documents of the War of 1812*, by the same author, in the Champlain Society publications.

Observe the high collars, reaching to the ears, worn by superior officers, especially Americans, and the cocked hats, worn broadside. Also note that the faces were clean shaven, except for a very small crescent-shaped side whisker. British officers wore the traditional scarlet coat, with a crimson sash around the waist and knotted at the left. American officers' uniforms were dark blue, and lacked the sash.

Page 175

Fort Wellington is situated on the eastern outskirts of Prescott, Ont., on the St. Lawrence. It is an excellent specimen of the earthwork and palisaded fortifications of the period, and remains as it was when completed in 1837. A small museum in one of its buildings contains some interesting military relics.

Page 178

The fight of Seven Oaks was the climax of the conflict between the rival fur-trading associations, the Hudson's Bay Company and the North-West Company.

Lord Selkirk had become one of the largest shareholders in the Hudson's Bay Company, and secured a grant of land on the Red River where in 1812 he established a colony of settlers from Scotland and Ireland. The Nor'westers and their Métis (French-Indian), hunters and trappers, fearing that settlement would destroy the fur-trade, opposed Selkirk's scheme. They harassed and drove away the settlers, demolished their buildings and almost exterminated the colony. Early in 1816 a body of half-breeds from Qu'Appelle and Portage la Prairie gathered for a raid on the settlement. On June 19th they approached Fort Douglas and the Colony Gardens. Governor Semple led a party out from the fort to intercept them. Semple's party was attacked, and all but six were killed. The total number killed was twenty-three, among them the Governor, his secretary, a doctor and a surgeon. The site, on the northern outskirts of the present city of Winnipeg, is marked by a monument.

The story is told in *The Red River Colony*, by L. A. Wood, in the Chronicles of Canada Series, and in works by Alexander Ross, George Bryce, and Professor Chester Martin. *Mine Inheritance*, a novel by Frederick Niven, gives an accurate and vivid picture of the time.

Page 180

See article on Rindisbacher in *The Beaver*, December, 1945.

Page 182

This mill, on Dedrick's Creek, about a mile and a half north of Port Rowan on Lake Erie, was built in 1808 on the site of a previous mill erected in 1798 by Jonathan Backhouse, who came from Yorkshire in 1791. It has always been in the possession of the family, who have been millers for five generations. It contains much of the early mechanism, the millstones, central shaft, crane, etc., though about 1894 modern roller equipment and turbine wheel were installed, by which it is operated today. It is an excellent specimen of the overshot wheel type.

Page 186

Colonel Talbot was a very important figure in the history of the settlement of south-western Upper Canada. His piquant personality, the striking contrast between his youth and his life in the backwoods, and his later years as the virtual ruler of the western peninsula make a story of unique and absorbing interest.

He belonged to the ancient Irish family of Talbot de Malahide, and was born in the ancestral castle near Dublin. He entered the army at an early age. With Arthur Wellesley, another young man, who became the Duke of Wellington, he was appointed aide to the Lord Lieutenant of Ireland. He served in Canada as secretary to Lieutenant-Governor Simcoe, 1792-1794, and accompanied him on his journey to Detroit, when he first saw the district which later he colonized. After some years of army service he abandoned European life and society and in 1801 settled in the wilderness on the shores of Lake Erie. He received large grants of land on which he placed settlers. Here he spent the remaining years of his life, varied by periodical visits to York, the Upper Canada capital, and an occasional trip to England and Ireland.

A full account of his life and the history of his settlement is given in *The Talbot Regime*, by C. O. Ermatinger, and further information in *The Talbot Papers*, by Dr. James H. Coyne, in the Transactions of the Royal Society of Canada, 1909.

The portrait depicts him at about the age of seventy, to judge from the costume, which is that of the eighteen-forties. His face is full and florid. His trousers are of homespun, with broad stripes of red and black.

Descriptions of his house are given in Dr. Coyne's paper referred to above, and in Mrs. Jameson's *Winter Studies and Summer Rambles in Canada*.

There are several descriptions of his appearance in contemporary accounts. In youth he is said to have been handsome and "quite a dandy"; but with advancing years he became corpulent. Mrs. Frances Stuart in *Our Forest Home* speaks of him as being fat and short. He persisted in wearing homespun garments of Port Talbot manufacture, even on his visits among aristocratic society in England. But he was especially noticeable for his famous greatcoat of yellow dyed sheepskin with the wool on, in which he was often seen driving Lady Sarah Maitland and Mrs. Gore, wives of Governors of Upper Canada, in his high box sleigh along King Street in York.

PART FOUR

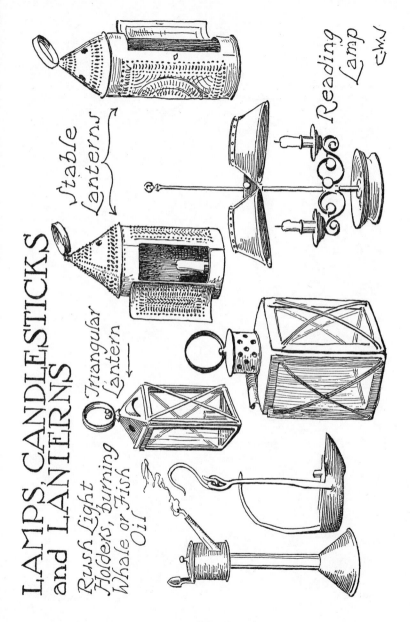

LAMPS, CANDLESTICKS and LANTERNS

Rush Light Holders, burning Whale or Fish Oil

Triangular Lantern

Stable Lanterns

Reading Lamp

C.W.J.

203

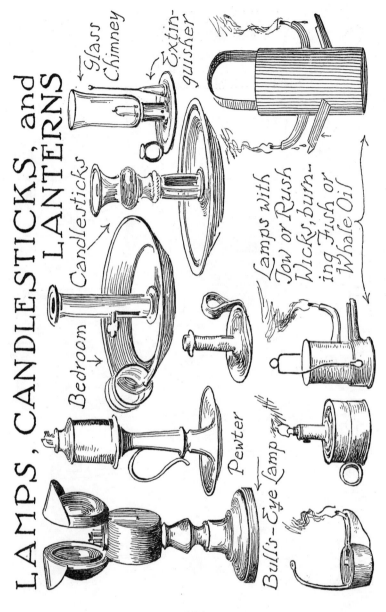

LAMPS, CANDLESTICKS, and LANTERNS

Glass Chimney

Extinguisher

Candlesticks

Bedroom

Lamps with Tow or Rush Wicks, burning Fish or Whale Oil

Pewter

Bull's-Eye Lamp

204

MORE LIGHT on the PAST

Sconce

Brass
Candlesticks
Silver
Tin

Candelabra
of Tin

Wall Sconce
All made

Bracket Sconces

c.W.J.

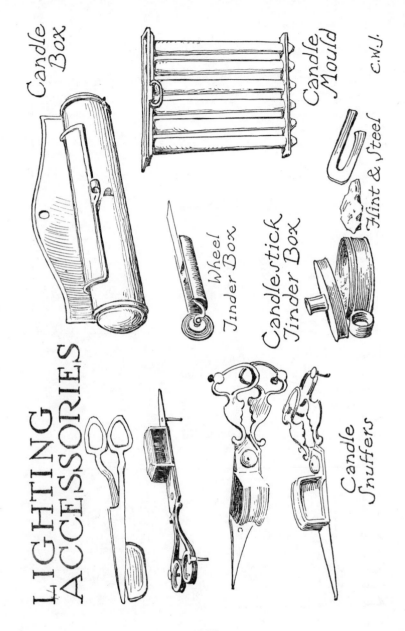

Candle Box

Candle Mould

C.W.J.

Flint & Steel

Wheel
Tinder Box

Candlestick
Tinder Box

LIGHTING
ACCESSORIES

Candle
Snuffers

UPPER CANADA DOORWAYS

Prest House, Queenston

On Dundas Road

1820

From Photos in "The Early Architecture of Ontario" by Prof. E. R. Arthur

Near Prescott

At Grimsby

Locust Hall St David's

207

EARLY HOUSES NIAGARA-ON-THE LAKE

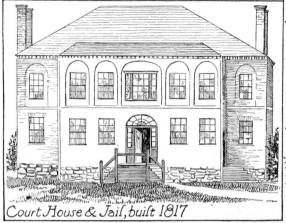

In this building Robert Gourlay was imprisoned for several months & tried for seditious attempt to promote disaffection to Government in 1819.

Here also in 1838 took place riot when escaped slave from the United States was rescued.

Court House & Jail, built 1817

House of Surveyor-General David W. Smith, no longer existing.

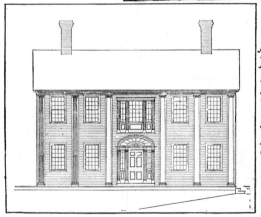

House of Colonel Ralph Clench, built after 1815.

From Measured Drawing by Wendell P. Lawson in "Small Houses of the late 18th & early 19th Centuries in Ontario."

UPPER CANADA METHODIST MEETING HOUSES

1st Methodist Chapel York. Built 1818. Corner King & Jordan Streets.

Red Meeting House Lundy's Lane Built 1817

Here 1st Canada Conference held, 1824.

Hallowell. Built 1829.

209

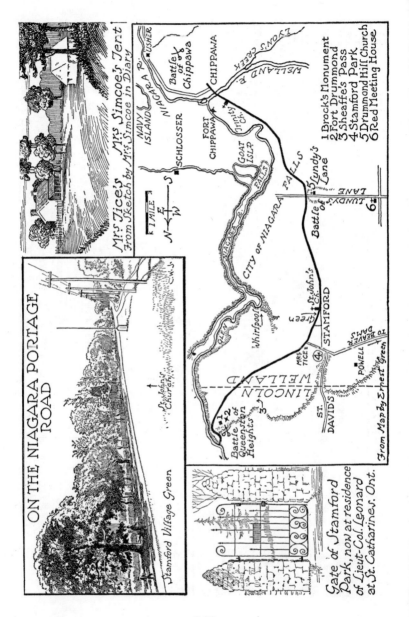

Mrs. Tice's   Mrs. Simcoe's Tent
From Sketch by Mrs. Simcoe in Diary

ON THE NIAGARA PORTAGE ROAD

Stamford Village Green

Gate of Stamford Park, now at residence of Lieut.-Col. Leonard at St. Catharines, Ont.

1 Brock's Monument
2 Fort Drummond
3 Sheaffe's Pass
4 Stamford Park
5 Drummond Hill Church
6 Red Meeting House

NAVY ISLAND
USHER
Battle of Chippawa
CHIPPAWA
LYON'S CREEK
NIAGARA R.
WELLAND R.
SCHLOSSER
FORT CHIPPAWA
Trinity Ch.
CHIPPAWA
GOAT ISL'D
FALLS
STILLS
Lundy's Lane
LUNDY'S LANE
Battle of
CITY OF NIAGARA FALLS
NIAGARA RIVER
St. John's Ch.
STAMFORD
Green
MRS. TICE
4
POWELL
TO BEAVER DAMS
ST. DAVID'S
LINCOLN   WELLAND
3
Battle of Queenston Heights
Whirlpool
GLEN
St. John's Church
From Map by Ernest Green

N   E
S   W
1 MILE

210

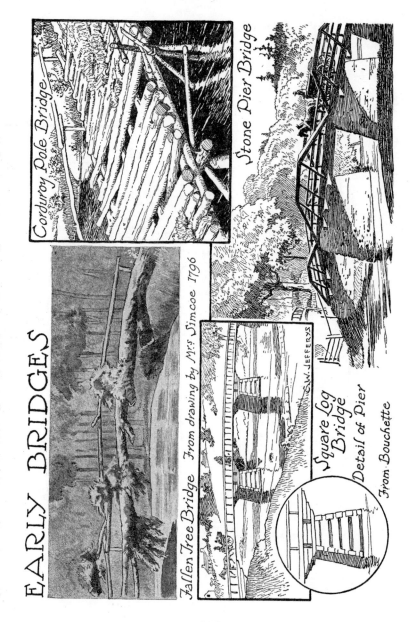

EARLY BRIDGES

Corduroy Pole Bridge

Stone Pier Bridge

Fallen Tree Bridge   From drawing by Mrs. Simcoe 1796

Square Log Bridge
Detail of Pier
From Bouchette

C.W. JEFFERYS

211

COVERED BRIDGE

TOLL GATE

C.W. JEFFERYS

THE CIRCUIT RIDER

213

THE ROYAL MAIL

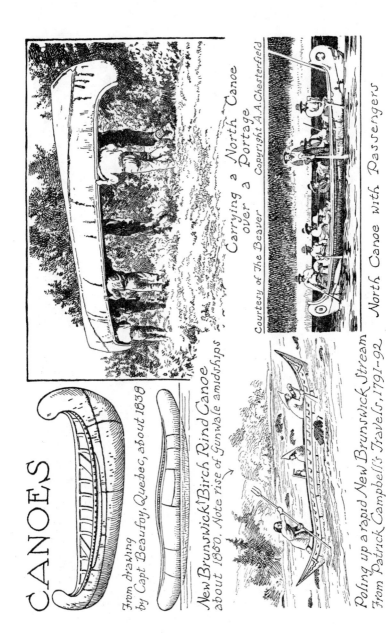

CANOES

From drawing
by Capt Beaufoy, Quebec, about 1838

New Brunswick Birch Rind Canoe
about 1860. Note rise of gunwale amidships

Carrying a North Canoe
over a Portage

Courtesy of The Beaver   Copyright A.A.Chesterfield

North Canoe with Passengers

Poling up a rapid New Brunswick stream
From Patrick Campbell's Travels, 1791-92

A LIGHT EXPRESS CANOE

on the way to FORT WILLIAM

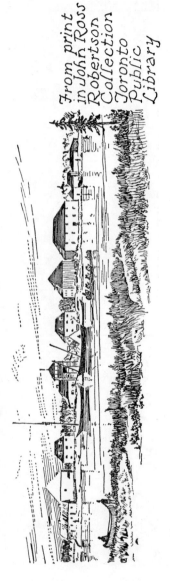

YORK BOATS

Under Sail

Polling up a shallow river

Courtesy of Hudson's Bay Co.

C.W. JEFFERYS

CARIOLES and SLEIGHS

About 1800

Cariole, about 1815

Officer's Sleigh 1826

Habitant's Wood Sleigh

At Fredericton 1835

About 1850

After Old Prints

From Krieghoff 1854

218

GOVERNORS of CANADA

Sir
John Coape Sherbrooke
1816
1818

Sir
James H. Craig
1807
1811

Earl of Dalhousie
1820
1828

Duke of
Richmond 1818-19

NEW BRUNSWICK PERSONAGES

Sir Howard Douglas.
Lieutenant Governor,
1824-1829.

Portrait taken some years
later Observe lower
coat collar & black
stock & cravat.
Simonds' portrait has
collar reaching to ears
& white cravat tied in
bow. Style of late 18th
Century

James Simonds.
One of the earliest
settlers at the
mouth of the
St. John
River.

Compare
portraits of
earlier N.S.
Judges, who
wore wigs &
ermine
trimmed
robes

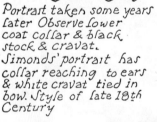

Hon. Ward
Chipman.
Chief
Justice

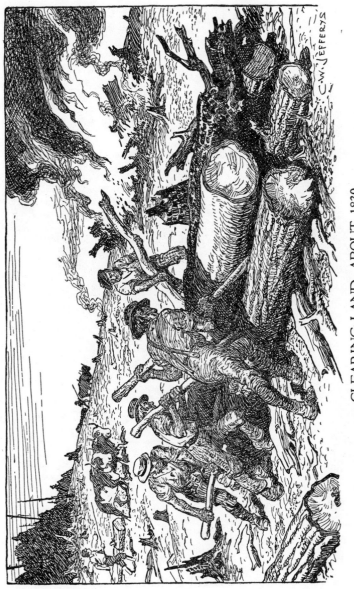

CLEARING LAND, ABOUT 1830

C.W. JEFFERYS

POTASH BOILING

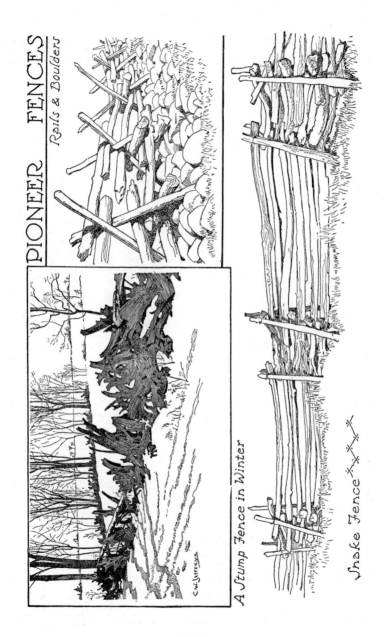

PIONEER FENCES

Rails & Boulders

A Stump Fence in Winter

Snake Fence

C.W.Jefferys

223

SHINGLE MAKING

K 21"

Maul for striking Frow

12" Frow

Splitting block with Frow

K 12 inches →

Draw Knife

Tapering Shingles with Draw Knife on Shaving Horse

C.W.J.

AGRICULTURAL IMPLEMENTS

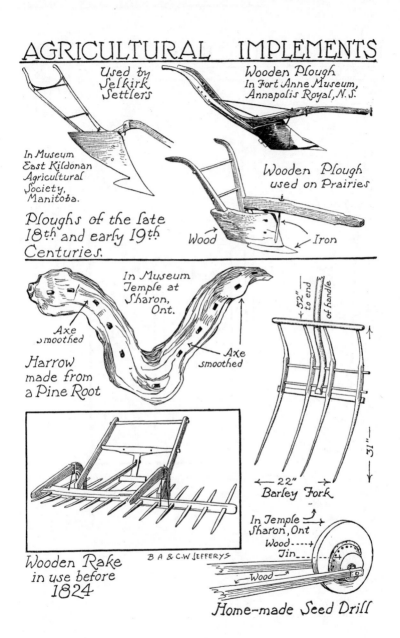

Used by Selkirk Settlers

Wooden Plough
In Fort Anne Museum,
Annapolis Royal, N.S.

In Museum
East Kildonan
Agricultural
Society,
Manitoba.

Ploughs of the late 18th and early 19th Centuries.

Wooden Plough used on Prairies

Wood

Iron

In Museum Temple at Sharon, Ont.

Axe smoothed

Axe smoothed

Harrow made from a Pine Root

52" to end of handle

31"

22"
Barley Fork

Wooden Rake in use before 1824

B A & C.W. JEFFERYS

In Temple Sharon, Ont.
Wood----
Tin----
----Wood----

Home-made Seed Drill

FARM TOOLS

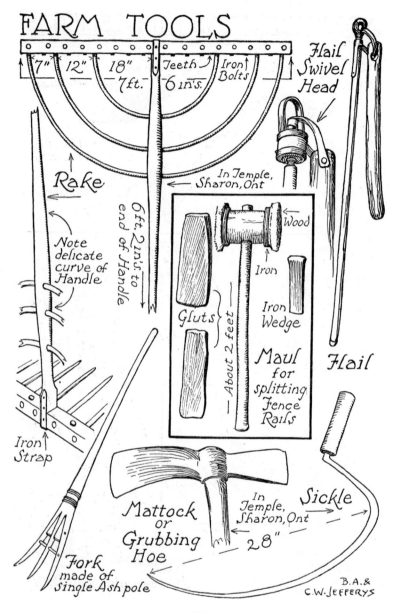

7" 12" 18" —Teeth— Iron Bolts
— 7 ft. — 6 in's.

Rake

Note delicate curve of Handle

6 ft. 2 in's. to end of Handle

In Temple, Sharon, Ont

Iron Strap

Fork made of single Ash pole

Flail Swivel Head

Wood

Iron

Iron Wedge

Gluts

About 2 feet

Maul for splitting Fence Rails

Flail

Mattock or Grubbing Hoe

In Temple, Sharon, Ont

28"

Sickle

B. A. & C. W. Jefferys

226

Threshing with Flail

Winnowing

THRESHING AND WINNOWING GRAIN

227

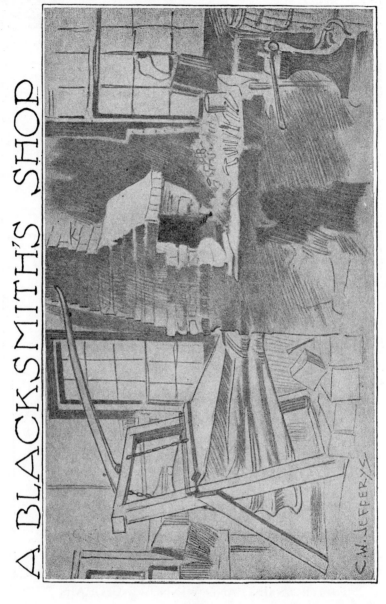

A BLACKSMITH'S SHOP

C.W.JEFFERYS

AROUND THE FARM

Log   Brick   Stone

Smoke Houses

Oaken Bucket   Covered Well

Corn Crib

Pole or Sweep Well

THE SPINNING WHEEL

EARLY MARITIME COLLEGES

King's College,
Windsor, 1791.

Dalhousie
College, Halifax, 1820.

King's College, now
University of New Brunswick
Fredericton, 1825~28.

PICTOU ACADEMY, N.S.

Thomas McCulloch, D.D

Academy Building, Opened 1818

C.W. JEFFERYS

Franklin on the Arctic Ocean,
1821   Based on drawing by
Lieut Back., R N.

Tattannaeuk
(Augustus) Eskimo Interpreter with Franklin, Back & Richardson

TOTEM POLES

Kwakiutl
Vancouver
Island

From
The Beaver
Courtesy
Hudson's Bay
Company

Haida Poles, Skidegate
Queen Charlotte Islands

WROUGHT IRONWORK

Typical Iron-barred Window of Quebec

Square-headed Nail

Section

Door Latches

Spikes with Angular & Round Hammered Heads

ASSOMPTION SASHES

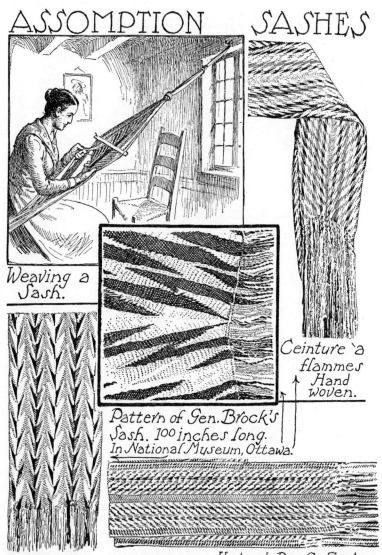

Weaving a
Sash.

Pattern of Gen. Brock's
Sash. 100 inches long.
In National Museum, Ottawa.

Ceinture 'a
flammes
Hand
woven.

Beaded Ceinture fléchée
Worn by Dr. Chenier, 1837.

Hudson's Bay Co. Trade
Sash. Machine woven.

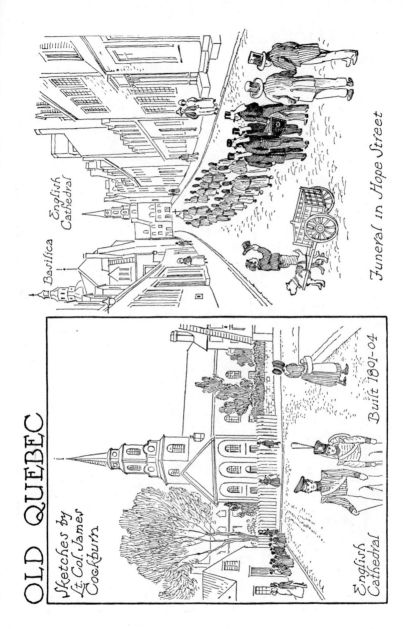

OLD QUEBEC

Sketches by
Lt. Col. James
Cockburn

English
Cathedral

Built 1801-04

Basilica

English
Cathedral

Funeral in Hope Street

The TEMPLE at SHARON, Ont.

One of the Four Doorways

Section of Exterior Boarding

David Willson, Founder, in old age

Temple of the Children of Peace

David Willson's Study

Interior, showing Jacob's Ladder for Choir.

ENGLISH CHURCHES of the TWENTIES

St. John the Evangelist
Stamford
Ont.

St. Thomas

C.W.JEFFERYS

239

FASHIONS IN TOMBSTONES

SACRED
TO THE MEMORY
OF
JONATHAN BATES
who died Aug. 11 1810
Aged 74 Years

SACRED
to the memory of
OBADIAH
JONES
Died Oct.r 5th 1812
Aged 29 Years

SACRED
To the
memory of
RICHARD
POINTER
who departed this

To the
memory of
DIANA
POINTER

1818

OBADIAH

1826

In Memory of
JOEL WILSON
Born in Co.Tyrone Ireland

1839

IN MEMORY OF
SIR FITZ-BONN CASTLE K.H.
LT. Col. of the Royal Engineers
Died at Kingston.
NOV. 2ND 1847.
AGED 55 YEARS.

...red Military Life in aton
of the British Governm.t
ric...s Parts of the Worl
g[?] and Fidelity Upwards
ALSO
...s Two Daughte...

1847

1855

240

OUTDOOR COMMUNION OF PRESBYTERIANS

241

HISTORICAL LANDMARKS
in and around HAMILTON, Ont.

Gates of Dundurn. Originally south entrance to estate of George Rolph at Dundas. Bought by Sir Allan MacNab & erected on present site in 1855.

At right → A Boundary Stone → on George Rolph estate, 1812

Mill at Crooks Hollow, 1813. From Photo by George Laidler, Esq.

Doorway of Mill.

GUARDIANS of the LAW

Constable's Baton

SCARBORO TP

Name of Township

Head of Tipstaff

Watchman calling the hour
"Past two o'clock and a stormy morning"

"In order to maintain the dignity of the court it was decided to procure 12 staves for the constables...the staves to be 7 feet in length & 1 inch & 3/4 thick, with the name of each township on each staff in plain legible letters."
Quotation from records of London District, in "The Talbot Regime", by Ermatinger

MALAHIDE TWP

Prisoner in Dock attended by Tipstaves

C.W JEFFERYS

EMIGRANTS IN THE WOODS

From drawing in possession of The Art Gallery of Toronto.

244

EMIGRANTS OF 1830

From Calendar of Toronto Art Students' League, 1900.

245

A COUNTRY DANCE, UPPER CANADA

NOTES ON PART FOUR

Page 207

In the better class early houses of Upper Canada the doorway was placed in the middle, and was designed in harmonious proportion with the building and constructed with fine craftsmanship. The door and its frame were of wood, carefully joined, and moulded and panelled with subtle refinement. Before 1840 these wooden door frames were generally set into an elliptical stone arch, which crowned a glass fanlight of a simple and delicate pattern. Many had side panels of glass to give additional light to the entrance hall.

The Prest House was built in 1818. For over eighty years it has been in the possession of the same family, who have kept it in its original condition and in excellent preservation. It is a good specimen of the Queenston limestone house.

"Locust Hall," St. David's, was built in 1820, and has been owned and occupied by the Woodruff family for three generations. They have appreciated the fine architectural qualities of their house, and it has been kept intact and in harmony with its period. The walls are built of bricks (smaller than those of today), laid in Flemish bond fashion, i.e. alternate "headers" and "stretchers," sides and ends; with stone quoins at the corners, and stone lintels and sills for the windows.

Page 208

A full account of Gourlay's life and of his trial is given in *Robert Fleming Gourlay*, by Justice W. R. Riddell, in Vol. XIV, Ontario Historical Society, Papers and Records.

In *Travels through part of the United States and Canada in 1818-1819*, by John M. Duncan, Vol. II, pp. 107-8, is a description of the jail. It was on the lower floor, "the cells surround and open from the hall, which leads to the court room. The partitions and doors of the cells are composed of pieces of oak firmly bolted together; the doors are about 9 inches thick, consisting of 2 thicknesses of wood with a sheet of iron between them. Some of the debtors' apartments have a small window, but the criminals have no light but from a small semi-circular opening in the doors. Debtors' cells have fire-places, but criminals have only a stove in the hall, from which no perceptible warmth can reach them."

The building was used as a court house and jail until 1847: from that date until 1862 as a jail only. In 1869 it was bought by Miss Rye, who established in it a home for orphan English girls, and as such was occupied for twenty-five years.

Page 209

Most of the early Methodist Meeting Houses were very humble wooden buildings of log or frame and clapboard construction. Few of them survive today. Many succumbed to fire or decay, while others were torn down to make way for larger and more permanent buildings on the same sites. Other early meeting houses are shown on a previous page in this volume.

The Red Meeting House at the extremity of Lundy's Lane west of the battle ground of 1814 was the scene of a dramatic episode six years later. The war had interrupted the connection with the American Church, but in 1820 a Conference was held here which was attended by over a hundred preachers, several of them from the United States. The congregation was too large for the meeting house, and the afternoon meeting was held in an adjoining grove. Twenty candidates were ordained as ministers. Carroll, in his *Case and his Cotemporaries*, states that Elder Case said that some of these young men who had taken part on opposite sides in the battles of Chippewa and Lundy's Lane now knelt together to receive their ordination. At the close of the service they were to be seen "locked in each others' arms and shedding tears of fond affection."

The site of the first Methodist Meeting House in York is now occupied by the towering structure of the Canadian Bank of Commerce building, which also covers the ground where for several years after 1845 the premises of the Toronto *Globe* were situated.

Page 210

The portage past Niagara Falls, until after the Revolutionary War, was on the east side of the river. By about 1789 a new road was opened and in use from Queenston to Chippewa, which became the route for all Canadian traffic. Maude in 1800 speaks of the large numbers of carts drawn by two yokes of oxen or two horses engaged in taking up bales and boxes and bringing down packs of furs. It was an important highway for troops, artillery and supplies during the War of 1812 and the Rebellion of 1837. The hard times of 1837, the competition of the Welland Canal and later of the railway brought the decline of the road. Full information concerning its history is given in an article by Ernest Green in *Vol. 23, Ontario Historical Society, Papers and Records*.

Stamford is said to have the only village green in Canada; here were held holiday sports, country fairs and militia musters. The Church of St. John the Evangelist, facing the green, was opened in 1825. It was erected largely by subscriptions from half-pay officers and English gentlemen living in the neighbourhood. Among them was the Lieutenant-Governor, Sir Peregrine Maitland, who purchased in 1822 the beautiful estate of Stamford Park, situated on the brow of the Queenston-St. David's escarpment. The house contained twenty-two rooms, luxuriously furnished. Mrs. Jameson visited it in 1837, and described it as "an elegant English villa with ornamented grounds, combined with some of the wildest and grandest features of the forest scene." The house was later burned and all trace of it has disappeared in the changes which the country has undergone, though the gates of the estate have been salvaged and are now in St. Catharines.

Mrs. Tice was the widow of Major Gilbert Tice, a Loyalist leader of Indians, and associate of Joseph Brant. She lived in the house, probably one of the best in the vicinity, for many years after his death. There are several references to it in the *Diary of Mrs. Simcoe*, who spent a fortnight there in August, 1793, occupying two rooms, with a tent for her servants. She says there was plenty of shade and cool air, when there was intense heat at Navy Hall at the mouth of the river. There is frequent mention of Mrs. Tice's house during the War of 1812. The dates of the deaths and the place of burial of both her husband and herself are unknown, and nothing remains of the house.

Page 211

In the early days of Canadian settlement the larger rivers were crossed by ferries. Generally it was not until population centred in villages and towns that bridges of any size or solidity were constructed.

The smaller streams, where they were shallow enough, were crossed by fording. Where gullies interposed or the creeks were too deep, fallen trees were used as foot bridges. Mrs. Simcoe's drawing shows Playter's bridge over the Don near Castle Frank. In her *Diary* she speaks of it thus: "It is a butternut tree fallen across the river, the branches still growing full leaf. Mrs. Playter, being timorous, a pole was fastened through the branches to hold by. Having attempted to pass it, I was determined to proceed, but was frightened before I got half way."

As the forest trails grew into rough roads, wider bridges were built of poles or saplings laid crosswise, corduroy fashion, on tree trunks supported by posts driven into the bed of the stream. Sometimes these pole bridges were covered with evergreen brush, sods and earth; but they were always insecure and often dangerous. The poles rotted, or broke, leaving gaps and holes which threatened man and horse with lame or broken legs. Spring freshets washed off the poles and earth, and often swept away the bridge entirely.

More substantial bridges were built of planks resting on piers of squared hewn logs dovetailed at the corners, as in log house construction, built high and stout to resist the drive and pressure of flood-borne ice. The illustration is from a drawing made by Bouchette about 1830 of a bridge over the river at St. Hyacinthe.

Of later construction were bridges of wooden beams and planks supported by stone piers. In the specimen illustrated, the bridge consists of three sections, the approaches inclining upward to a middle span. The piers, of flat stones from the river bed, were built high and strong enough to be beyond the reach of the freshets which often flooded the flats of the wide river valley, and to withstand the impact of the ice in the spring break-up.

The now almost extinct covered bridge is shown on page 212.

Page 216

The picture of the light express canoe is from an old water colour in the possession of the Museum of the Hudson's Bay Company, Winnipeg, by whose courtesy it is here reproduced.

It shows two officers seated amidships, and in the stern are seen a kettle and two ladles used in boiling pitch, and a roll of birch bark, for mending the canoe if damaged on the voyage.

Page 217

York boats were built of selected spruce and shaped like whale boats, the bow and stern pointed at an angle of forty-five degrees. They were fitted with a rudder and a removable mast, which when not in use was sometimes slung alongside, as shown in the drawing. They were of various sizes, from twenty-eight feet to forty feet in length. The larger boats carried about one hundred "pieces," or packages of ninety pounds, in comparison with the "Canoes du Nord," which carried only twenty-five. They were equipped with duck canvas covers for protecting the goods in wet weather, and with ropes for hauling over the portages on rollers.

The crew of the larger boats consisted of ten men: a steersman, or captain, a bowsman with a long pole to fend the boat off rocks, and eight middlemen, who rowed with heavy sweeps, twenty feet long, rising to their feet on the pull of the oars, and sitting down to complete the stroke. When the wind was favourable and the water smooth, the mast was hoisted and fitted with a square sail.

York boats were used to some extent in 1795 on the Saskatchewan River, from Edmonton to Lake Winnipeg. By 1820-1826 they were in common use wherever the depth of the water admitted, on the main Hudson's Bay Company routes.

See *The Honourable Company*, by Douglas MacKay, and article by John Peter Turner, in *The Beaver*, December, 1943.

Page 218

In this page, as in others, the limits of the period covered generally by this volume have been exceeded. This has been done in order to show some of the changes in style which the sleigh has undergone during the last century.

The sketches are taken from early Canadian prints, many of which depict sleighing scenes.

Officers of the British Army stationed at Canadian garrisons organized sleigh clubs and held driving parades through the towns and the adjacent country, accompanied by their wives and the ladies of the locality. The officers vied with each other in fine horses and handsome sleighs, which sometimes bore on their sides the coats-of-arms of their owners. Robes of bear or buffalo fur protected them from the cold. Tandem teams were fashionable.

The earlier sleighs had low-seated bodies resting on heavy wooden runners shod with iron. Cariole was the French-Canadian name for these vehicles. The habitants brought their produce to market on heavy wooden sledges, furnished with upright stakes at the sides roped together to hold bags of grain, cordwood, or bales of hay, often surmounted by the frozen carcasses of pigs, and drawn by a single shaggy-coated Canadian pony. Innkeepers on the main roads kept relays of post horses for travellers.

In time the body of the sleigh and the seats were elevated on straight iron supports above the iron runners, until they reached a height that made upsets frequent. About 1850 the supports took graceful curves, as may be seen in Krieghoff's prints and paintings, which show the wide varieties of shapes used by all classes.

Page 221

Observe the details of the dress of the men at work in contrast to that of the Loyalist pioneers. Those in this illustration belong to the later immigration of the eighteen-twenties and thirties, as shown by the stiff high-crowned hats of felt or straw, the loose corduroy trousers, tied below the knee, and the ankle-high boots.

Graphic descriptions of the burning of the log heaps are given in the books by Mrs. Moodie, Mrs. Traill, Major Strickland, and other writers.

Page 224

Shingles were usually made of cedar. Blocks of the required width (about five inches), and generally about eighteen inches long, were cut from the log, and placed upright in the fork of the Frow Horse. The workman, seated on the Horse, set the blade of the Frow across the top of the block, and struck the projecting end with a Club or Maul. As the Frow penetrated the block, he wiggled the handle, which was set loosely in its socket, until the "shake," as the untrimmed shingle was called, flew off. This proceeding was repeated until the whole block was split into slabs of uniform thickness. The shake was then placed in the clamp of a Shaving Horse, as shown in the drawing, and tapered by the Draw Knife toward one side of the shingle and to the end nearest the workman, to allow for overlapping. The surface of these hand-made shingles followed the grain of the wood, which shed more easily rain and melting snow, prevented the moisture entering the fibres of the wood and thus made them last longer.

Page 229

In the Lawson Memorial Library, University of Western Ontario, London is the MS. of a thesis on *Pioneer Art and Architecture*, by C. S. Buck, consisting of several volumes, profusely illustrated by drawings, plans and photographs by the author. It is a most comprehensive study of the subject, especially as relating to Western Ontario. Some of the drawings in this volume are based on data gathered from this invaluable source, which should be consulted by all seeking detailed information on early handicrafts and methods of construction.

The smoke house, an indispensable adjunct to the farm, was generally built conveniently near the dwelling. Here legs, shoulders and sides of pork and beef were hung in the smudge from smouldering sticks of beech, birch, hickory or maple, or from corn cobs. The meat after being smoked was covered with a linen or cotton cloth and given a coat of whitewash.

Corncribs were set about a couple of feet above the ground on posts, with walls of narrow boards set upright an inch or so apart to permit a free circulation of air. The wide roof and overhanging eaves shed the rain clear of the walls. The ripe ears of corn were stored in these receptacles to dry.

Page 232

Thomas McCulloch (1777-1843), born in Scotland, educated at Glasgow University, came to Nova Scotia in 1803 as minister of the Presbyterian church at Pictou. He took a great interest in popular education, and was foremost in the foundation of Pictou Academy. Practical and scientific subjects were emphasized in its curriculum, and a museum of natural history was established. In 1838 Dr. McCulloch became the first president of Dalhousie College.

See *An introduction to the history of Dalhousie University,* by D. C. Harvey.

Page 233

The drawing of Tattannaeuk is in the Museum of the Hudson's Bay Co., Winnipeg.

Page 234

Totem poles are found on the North Pacific Coast, among the Haida, the Tsimsyan and the Kwakiutl tribes. They are of two types—house poles and memorial poles. House poles were heraldic signs, symbolizing family ancestry and tribal myths and traditions. They were erected in front of the houses, the entrance to which was sometimes through them. Memorial poles, in use particularly among the Tsimsyan, commemorated deceased members of the family, and were erected at some distance from the house.

These tall open-air poles were of later date than the carved interior posts described by the early explorers, Cook and Meares, and depicted by Webber, as shown in previous pages in this volume. None of the early views show poles outside the houses. The exterior poles were generally more delicately and elaborately carved. This was made possible by metal tools obtained from white traders.

Dr. Marius Barbeau has made an intensive study of these poles, and his numerous articles and monographs give the most complete and authoritative information on the subject. See also articles in *The Beaver* for June, 1940, and September, 1942, which contain many illustrations, some of which have been copied in this volume.

Page 236

Assomption Sash, by Marius Barbeau, a bulletin issued by *The National Museum of Canada, Ottawa,* gives full information on these sashes, their origin, history and method of weaving, with many illustrations. The author is the leading authority on French-Canadian handicrafts, and his monograph is based on years of research among old records, and the detailed examination of numerous specimens.

The art of weaving these sashes was almost lost when in 1907 the Canadian Handicrafts Guild of Montreal exhibited several of them, and engaged Mme. Venne, one of the few surviving hand weavers, to give a public demonstration of their manufacture. Dr. E. Z. Massicotte became interested and took the initiative in their preservation, and with Dr. Barbeau aroused a revival of interest in this interesting handicraft. Thanks to their efforts the technique is now being taught in the handicraft schools, and hand-woven sashes are now being made in various parts of the province.

Page 237

Lieutenant-Colonel James Cockburn was stationed in Canada for several years, during which he made a great number of water colour drawings. Some of these were reproduced and published as colour prints, but they are only a small portion of the many sketches he produced in Canada. The Manoir Richelieu Collection at Murray Bay contains a number of original drawings, in addition to sets of his prints. The Sigmund Samuel Collection possesses over a hundred originals, which depict scenes from the St. Lawrence to the Niagara.

His drawings give most valuable details of early buildings and show the general appearance of the country at the period. Especially interesting are the human figures which he introduces into his scenes: they are always in character with the localities depicted, and are faithful transcripts of the costumes and uniforms, whether soldiers, sailors, ladies and gentlemen, habitants, voyageurs or pioneer settlers.

The sketch of the English Cathedral is possibly the earliest drawing of this building that exists.

The drawing of the funeral procession gives a view looking up the present Ste. Famille Street from near Hope Gate, which at that time gave its name to the street. Besides being an excellent sketch of the buildings, several of which still survive, it is especially valuable for the details of the funeral cortège, which is evidently drawn from observation. The funeral is that of a young person, as is indicated by the small size of the coffin and the white bands around the hats of the bearers, a detail which shows that this custom is of greater antiquity than is popularly supposed.

M. P. G. Roy, archivist-emeritus of the Province of Quebec, always most generous in his assistance to historical inquirers, has kindly supplied information regarding old French-Canadian funeral customs. I translate freely his remarks. "I have examined with keen interest Cockburn's drawing. . . . In the olden time, when a person died not too far from the church, the clergy proceeded to the house of mourning to make what was called 'la levée du corps,' and accompanied the body to the church where the service was to be performed. In the case of Cockburn's drawing the house of the deceased evidently was in Ste. Famille Street and near the Cathedral. The cross at the head of the cortège shows that those who precede the coffin are clergy, wearing the 'camail,' or cape, and the large 'barrette' or headdress of the early days. That they are priests or members of religious orders is also proved by the fact that they wear no crepe as do the bearers. The clergy always walked in front of the coffin. It is probable that owing to lack of space Cockburn shows only a small portion of the procession which followed it. . . . It is a most interesting drawing."

Both of these sketches are included by the courtesy of the owner, Sigmund Samuel, Esq., LL.D.

Page 238

The Temple at Sharon, Ont., was built by David Willson (1777-1866) and the members of the sect founded by him. Willson belonged to the Society of Friends but seceded from that body in 1812, and organized a religious community known as the Children of Peace. While retaining some of the Quaker doctrines, the new religion established a richer and more picturesque form of worship, based on a mixture of mysticism and Jewish ceremonial. Music was cultivated and formed a large part of their services, and the white-robed Sharon choir, its organ, and its silver band became more than locally famous. The arts of architecture and painting found expression in the building and decoration of the Meeting House (now demolished), in Willson's study, and especially in the Temple, a sixty feet square wooden structure of three storeys, of unique and original design. These two buildings have been preserved, and are owned and maintained by the York Pioneer and Historical Society, which has installed in the Temple a museum containing many interesting specimens of farm tools and articles of domestic use.

The story of the Children of Peace is well told in Prof. A. G. Dorland's *History of the Society of Friends (Quakers) in Canada.* Earlier descriptions of the sect, its buildings and its founder, are given in Rev. H. Scadding's *Toronto of Old*, in *The History of the County of York*, and in W. L. Mackenzie's *Sketches of Canada and the United States.*

Page 239

The decade from 1820 to 1830 was marked by the erection of numerous buildings of the Church of England in western Upper Canada, of which St. John's, Stamford, erected in 1825, is a typical specimen. That at St. Thomas dates from 1824.

Page 240

The earliest settlers buried their dead in small plots on their farms. The graves were marked by wooden slabs or roughly shaped stones on which brief inscriptions, often only initials and dates, were crudely scratched. In course of time the wooden markers decayed, the stones were broken, and today few of these first memorials remain, and many of these early burial plots are indicated only by the low grave mounds.

As population increased churches provided community burial grounds. Stone masons, established in the towns and villages, began to supply more smoothly finished grave-stones of simple design.

During the period from about 1770 to the eighteen-thirties the inscriptions were incised with Roman lettering, and an occasional line of slanting Italic, the letters generally well shaped and harmoniously spaced. Sometimes, however, the carver's miscalculation made it necessary for him to diminish the size of the last few letters and crowd them together to finish the line. This feature occurs frequently in the stones of this period. A simple carving in low relief often ornamented the head of the stone; an urn, a weeping willow, a hand with heaven-pointing finger were favourite emblems.

About 1830-1840 rather clumsy raised block lettering came into fashion. Decoration became more elaborate and the tombstones lost the simplicity, harmonious proportions and graceful delicacy that marked the earlier incised stones. From then until well into the eighteen-eighties tombstone fashions became progressively pretentious, and echo the bad taste that characterized the house decoration and furniture of the period.

Page 241

In pioneer days, especially in Nova Scotia, before churches were built, the Presbyterians of a neighbourhood gathered to partake of the Communion in some convenient place in the open air, often in a clearing in the woods. People came from great distances to these meetings, notice of which had been sent throughout the country. A description of these gatherings is given in Patterson's *History of Pictou*.

Page 242

The gates of Dundurn once formed the entrance to the estate of George Rolph at Dundas, Ont. In 1855 Allan MacNab purchased them from him and brought them to Dundurn. The iron gates were made in England, but the pillars and wall were cut from Dundas Mountain stone. On the inside of the entrance is a tablet bearing the inscription: "John Allen, Stone Cutter, Staffordshire, England. Emigrated to Canada in 1820. In 1828 he constructed these pillars and erected this monument, that he lived and will die a faithful subject to his King and Country, and proud of his national birth."

The stone marked G.R. is one of several along the York Road (originally Dundas Street). The initials have been wrongly supposed to represent *Georgius Rex;* but really are those of George Rolph, who thus marked the boundary of his property. The stones are set upright well into the ground, the letters being about four inches high. A similar stone is to be seen in the neighbourhood marked R.H. No. 3, indicating the boundary of the property of Richard Hatt.

Crooks' Hollow is situated near Greenville, on the creek which flows over Webster's Falls of today. It takes its name from James Crooks, a leading merchant of Upper Canada, who made a settlement here about 1800. Mills were erected, and industries flourished until the water power failed. Here was established a mill, to which was awarded a bonus for turning out the first sheet of paper manufactured in Upper Canada. All that remains of it today is the stone foundation of a barn. Helliwell, the man who ran it, also established a paper mill on the Don, north of Toronto.

For information on these landmarks I am indebted to Messrs. Melville Bailey and Roy Woodhouse.

Page 244

A period of depression in Great Britain followed the cessation of the Napoleonic war. The army was reduced, and many officers were retired on half-pay. Farm labourers, artisans, small tradesmen, gentry, soldiers and civilians all felt the pinch of hard times. Many sought relief by emigrating to North America, and throughout the years of the twenties and thirties a flood of newcomers poured into Canada. Among them were many gentlefolk, accustomed to the comforts and refinements of the old land, who found life in the backwoods painful, difficult and discouraging. Some succumbed in the struggle, but many also resolutely set themselves to the task of building a new life for themselves and their children, and succeeded in establishing comfortable homes and prosperous communities. The drawing attempts to express the situation of these people set down in the midst of the lonely wilderness, as it is poignantly described in such books as Mrs. Moodie's *Roughing it in the bush*, Mrs. Traill's *Backwoods of Canada*, and Mrs. Stewart's *Our Forest Home.*

APPENDIX

BIBLIOGRAPHY AND SOURCES OF INFORMATION

Many of the sources given in Vol. I of *The Picture Gallery of Canadian History* contain much that relates also to the period covered by this volume. They are not repeated herein. The list, especially that of the bibliography, does not pretend to be complete. It includes those which I have found most useful. Hence many sources indispensable to the detailed knowledge of other topics in Canadian history are omitted.

An acquaintance with the political and constitutional development of the country, however, is necessary as a basis for the proper understanding and the true and complete representation of its social life. Without this, no amount of special knowledge of details will convey the right historical and artistic atmosphere, or the connection of the subject depicted with its period. Lacking this pervading sense of the time-spirit, many otherwise admirable works, literary, pictorial and dramatic, remain only "costume pieces." I am keenly conscious that many of my own attempts at imaginative pictorial reconstruction attain only this outward appearance, and fail to express the inner significance. I must be content if they arouse an interest that will lead to further study.

I. General Works

Canada: H. E. Egerton.

History of Canada (1763-1812): C. P. Lucas.

The Making of Canada: A. G. Bradley.

Canada, The Foundations of Its Future: S. Leacock.

British Emigration to British North America: Helen G. Cowan. 1928.

The Canadians: G. M. Wrong.

Dominion of the North: D. G. Creighton.

II. Unpublished Manuscripts

"D. W. Smith Papers": Toronto Public Library.

"Jarvis Papers": Toronto Public Library.

"Powell Papers": Toronto Public Library.

"Laurent Quetton St. George Papers": Toronto Public Library.

"Letters of Mrs. Martin Hunter": Transcripts by G. H. Markham, Saint John, N.B.

"Journal of Sir Martin Hunter": Transcripts by G. H. Markham, Saint John, N.B.

"Inventory of Furniture, etc., of the Late Sir William Johnson": Transcripts by Mrs. Celia File.

"Journal of York Factory, 1787": Transcripts by C. W. Jefferys.

"Journal of Fort Severn, and Letters, 1783": Transcripts by C. W. Jefferys.

"Cartwright Papers": Douglas Library, Queen's University.

"Garrison Orders, etc., Fort Niagara, 1812-13": Douglas Library, Queen's University.

"De Salaberry Papers": Archives of Canada, Ottawa.

"Haldimand Papers": Archives of Canada, Ottawa.

"Pictures of Canadian Military Events, etc.": A. Sandham. Archives of Canada, Ottawa.

III. REPRINTS OF DOCUMENTS, LETTERS, ETC.

Journals of the Siege of Quebec, 1775-76: Literary and Historical Society of Quebec.

The Winslow Papers, 1776-1826: Edited by Rev. W. O. Raymond.

Journey . . . to the Northern Ocean, 1769-72. Samuel Hearne: Edited by J. B. Tyrrell. (Champlain Society)

Nova Scotia Documents: Atkins.

Travels in . . . North America, 1793. Patrick Campbell: Edited by H. H. Langton and W. F. Ganong. (Champlain Society)

Diary of Mrs. Simcoe: Edited by J. Ross Robertson.

Correspondence of Lt. Gov. J. G. Simcoe: Ontario Historical Society.

The Russell Papers: Ontario Historical Society.

Journal of Capt. James Colnett aboard the Argonaut, 1789-91: Edited by F. W. Howay. (Champlain Society)

Documentary History of the War of 1812: Edited by E. Cruikshank. (Lundy's Lane Historical Society)

Select Documents of the War of 1812: Edited by William Wood. (Champlain Society)

Documents relating to the North West Company: Edited by W. S. Wallace. (Champlain Society)

Narrative of David Thompson's Explorations: Edited by J. B. Tyrrell. (Champlain Society)

Colin Robertson's Letters, 1817-22: Edited by E. E. Rich. (Champlain Society)

Minutes of Council of Northern Department 1821-23: Edited by R. H. Fleming. (Champlain Society)

Hargrave Correspondence, 1821-43: Edited by G. de T. Glazebrook. (Champlain Society)

Twenty-Five Years' Service with the Hudson's Bay Company. John McLean. Edited by W. S. Wallace. (Champlain Society)

Simpson's Athabasca Journal: Edited by E. E. Rich. (Champlain Society)

> The foregoing works and others concerning the fur trade of the northwest, published by The Champlain Society are ably edited, copiously annotated, and give many valuable details regarding equipment, goods, methods of transportation, canoe routes, etc.

Les Bourgeois de la Compagnie du Nord-Ouest: Masson.

Hadfield's Diary. 1785.

Travels and Adventures in Canada and the Indian Territories, 1760-'96. Alexander Henry: Edited by James Bain.

> Description of Massacre at Michilimackinac.

IV. CONTEMPORARY WORKS, EXPLORATION AND TRAVEL

Voyage to the Pacific Ocean: James Cook. 1784.

Voyage of Discovery: G. Vancouver. 1798.

Travels: Duc de La Rochefoucault Liancourt. 1799.

Tour in Upper and Lower Canada: J. C. Ogden. 1799.

Travels: Isaac Weld. 1800.

Voyages: Alexander Mackenzie. 1801.

Travels through the Canadas: G. Heriot. 1807.

> Contains excellent illustrations and gives details of the life of the period as also does

Travels: John Lambert. 1808.

Letters from Canada: H. Gray. 1809.

Topographical Description of Lower Canada, with remarks upon Upper Canada: J. Bouchette. 1815.

Travels in the United States and Canada: Duncan. 1818.

Travels in Canada and the United States: F. Hall. 1818.

The Shoe and Canoe: J. J. Bigsby. 1850.

> This book, though not published till many years later, deals with the period covered by this volume. It gives graphic descriptions of voyageur life, and of the condition of the country and its people in general. It contains several engravings of scenery.

Journal of Voyages and Travels: D. W. Harmon. 1820.

> Life as a fur trader in the North-West.

Substance of a Journal: Rev. John West.

> Selkirk Settlement, and Indian missions in the Maritimes.

Statistical Account of Upper Canada: R. F. Gourlay. 1822.

Hints to Emigrants: W. Bell. 1824.

Five Years' residence in the Canadas: E. A. Talbot. 1824.

> Information on the Talbot Settlement.

Sketches of Upper Canada: Howison. 1825.

Personal Narrative of Travels: De Roos. 1826-27.

Three Years in Canada: John MacTaggart.

> Graphic descriptions of country and people. Author worked on Rideau Canal survey.

Twenty-Seven Years in Canada West: Strickland. 1853.

> Gives information regarding settlement life in Upper Canada during the period.

Travels in North America: Basil Hall. 1829.

Forest Scenes: Sir George Head. 1829.

V. SPECIAL TOPICS, PERIODS AND LOCALITIES

The Great Migration: E. C. Guillet.

> Contains illustrations from contemporary sources.

History of the Settlement of Upper Canada: W. Canniff. 1869.

> Contains much material on Loyalists.

Upper Canada Sketches: Conant.

Country Life in Canada: Canniff Haight.

History of Lennox and Addington: W. S. Herrington.

British Emigration to British North America: Helen Cowan.

Pioneer Life in Upper Canada: A. B. Sherk.
> Many photographic illustrations.

The Province of Ontario: J. E. Middleton and Fred Landon.

Pioneers of Old Ontario: W. L. Smith.
> Reminiscences and traditions.

Lake Huron: Fred Landon.

Our Struggle for the Fourteenth Colony: Justin Smith.
> American Invasion of Canada, 1775-6.

Un Général Allemand au Canada: Georges Monarque.
> Information on Riedesel and German mercenaries in Revolutionary War.

Life of Joseph Brant: W. L. Stone.

Castorologia, or History and Traditions of the Canadian Beaver:
H. T. Martin.

Five Fur Traders of the North West: Grace Lee Nute and G. M.
Gates.

The North West Company: G. C. Davidson.

The Fur Trade: H. A. Innis.

Freshwater: G. A. Cuthbertson.
> Many pictures of shipping on the Great Lakes.

Astoria: Washington Irving.

Narrative: Gabriel Franchère.

Adventures and Sufferings: John Jewitt.
> These three books deal with the Pacific Coast.

Narrative of Journey to the Polar Sea: John Franklin.

Letters from Nova Scotia: W. Moorsom.

Historical and Statistical Account of Nova Scotia: T. C. Haliburton.

History of Nova Scotia: Beamish Murdoch.

The Medical Profession in Upper Canada, 1783-1850: W. Canniff.

Four Centuries of Medical History in Canada: J. J. Heagerty.

The Society of Friends in Canada: A. G. Dorland.

Case and his Cotemporaries: Carroll.

History of Methodism in Canada: Playter.

From Strachan to Owen: W. Perkins Bull.

From Macdonell to McGuigan: W. Perkins Bull.

These two books contain many portraits and other illustrations, and much information.

History of the Scotch Presbyterian Church, St. Gabriel Street, Montreal: Rev. Rob't. Campbell.

A Colony of Émigrés in Canada, 1798-1816: Lucy E. Textor.

History of the Post Office: W. Smith.

Memoires: P. A. de Gaspé.

Memoirs of Sir Isaac Brock: F. B. Tupper.

Isaac Brock: W. Nursey.

Tecumseh: N. S. Gurd.

Operations of the Right Division: John Richardson.

1812, the War and its Moral: V. Coffin.

The Story of the Nancy: C. H. J. Snider.

In the wake of the Eighteen Twelvers: C. H. J. Snider.

Journal of W. H. Merritt.

Stirring Incidents in the life of a British Soldier: T. Faughnan.

Ten Years of Upper Canada, 1805-15: M. Edgar.

Local histories are numerous. They contain much valuable material, but in some cases their information should be checked by reference to other sources. The following list includes only a few of the large number published.

Toronto of Old: Rev. C. Scadding.

Landmarks of Toronto: J. Ross Robertson.   (6 vols.)

History of the County of Pictou, N.S.: Rev. George Patterson.

Reminiscences of the Early History of Galt and Dumfries: James Young.

History of Niagara: Janet Carnochan.

Annals of Niagara: W. Kirby.

History of Kingston, Ont.: A. M. Machar.

Simcoe County: A. F. Hunter.

Leeds and Grenville: F. Leavitt.

Glengarry County: J. A. Macdonell.

Burford: Muir.
> Contains much information on early U.C. militia.

Brant County: F. W. Reville.

Dundas County: J. Croil.

Wentworth County: J. H. Smith.

Lennox and Addington: W. S. Herrington.

The Talbot Papers: James Coyne. Royal Society of Canada, 1909.

The Talbot Régime: C. O. Ermatinger.

In the Days of the Canada Company: Lizars.

The Perkins Bull Series on the History of *Peel County.*

Longueuil: Jodoin and Vincent.

The Seigneury of Lauzon: J. E. Roy.

St. Denis, Richelieu: Abbé J. B. A. Allaire.

Fergus: H. Templin.

History of Central New Brunswick: L. M. Beckwith Maxwell.

Montreal, under British Rule: W. H. Atherton.

> Many novels and poems on Canadian historical themes give a living picture of the past. They vary in their degree of accuracy as to details, but those in the following list may be considered as authentic in their general atmosphere. They are instructive also as representing the ideals and opinions of the periods in which they were written.

The Bastonnais: J. T. Lesperance. 1877.
> The American Invasion of Canada, 1775-6.

The History of Emily Montague: Frances Brooke. 1769.
> Written by the wife of the British Chaplain in Quebec, this first Canadian novel gives a vivid picture of the social life of the period. It has been reprinted under the editorship of Lawrence Burpee.

Wacousta: John Richardson.
> The siege of Detroit by Pontiac. Melodramatic and romantic, reflects the sentiments of the time.

The Canadian Brothers: John Richardson.
> On War of 1812.

The U.E.: William Kirby.
> Narrative poem on Loyalists, by the author of *The Golden Dog.*

Tecumseh: Charles Mair. 1886.
> Poetic drama on War of 1812.

Laura Secord: S. A. Curzon.
Drama on heroine of Beaver Dams.

The Old Judge: T. C. Haliburton.
Short stories and sketches of early Nova Scotia history.

Boughs Bend Over: M. Parlow French.

Thorn Apple Tree: Grace Campbell.
These two recent novels of early pioneer life in Ontario give intimate and authentic details and a convincing imaginative reconstruction of the period.

His Majesty's Yankees: T. H. Raddall.
A graphic presentation of Nova Scotia life at the period of the American Revolution.

Guns of Burgoyne: Bruce Lancaster.
Vivid and authentic. Remarkable for its lifelike characterization of Madame Riedesel and other personages of the Revolutionary Period.

Oliver Wiswell: Kenneth Roberts.

Sympathetic portrait of a Loyalist. Realistic view of the Revolution. Both these works by American authors show an understanding of the British and Canadian point of view. They are outstanding imaginative reconstructions of the past, based on extensive study of historical documents.

Récits d'Histoire Canadienne: E. Z. Massicotte.

Vielles Choses, Vielles Gens: G. Bouchard.

Le Duel au Canada: Ægidius Fauteux.

Old Province Tales, N.S.: A. MacMechan.

Old Province Tales, U.C.: W. R. Riddell.

Les Ecclésiastiques et les Royalistes Français réfugiés au Canada: N. E. Dionne.

Les Lettres Canadiennes d'autrefois: Seraphin Marion.

Artistes Peintres, canadiens-français: G. Bellevive.

The Chronicles of Canada Series and *The Makers of Canada* include several works relating to this period.

VI. Periodical Publications

In addition to the publications cited in Vol. I, those of the large number of historical societies throughout Canada should be consulted. It is impossible here to give a complete list, but among the most voluminous and informative may be mentioned.

Ontario Historical Society—*Papers and Records.*

Niagara Historical Society—*Publications*.

London and Middlesex Historical Society—*Transactions*.

Welland County Historical Society—*Papers and Records*.

Women's Canadian Historical Society, Toronto—*Transactions*.

Lennox and Addington Historical Society—*Papers and Records*.

Lawson Memorial Library, University of Western Ontario, London—*Western Ontario Historical Notes*.

New Brunswick Historical Society—*Publications*.

Nova Scotia Historical Society—*Publications*.

British Columbia Historical Quarterly.

Hudson's Bay Company—*The Beaver*.

Excellent illustrations, many historical articles.

VII. Museums and Libraries

Many of those mentioned in Vol. I contain pictures and objects connected with this period. Throughout the various provinces also there are numerous smaller museums with local collections. Public libraries often contain documents, letters, diaries, portraits, views and relics relating to their localities. This department of library work is receiving increasing attention, and many libraries now include a section devoted to local history. Some Women's Institutes also have gathered similar material. These collections are of varying degrees of importance and of convenience for inspection; many of them are cramped for space and lack sufficient financial support; but all should be examined in the quest for material indispensable to the graphic reconstruction of our past. Unexpected or long sought information is often to be found in these minor collections. They should never be ignored or overlooked, however heterogeneous and unimportant they may appear. Diligent search will sometimes reward the historical detective with the discovery of a unique and characteristic specimen or document. The number of these local repositories is so great that no attempt can be made here to compile a complete directory of them. Some are mentioned in the notes. Others wherein I have found useful material are included in the following list:

Fort York, Toronto, Ont.

Fort George, Niagara-on-the-Lake, Ont.

FORT ERIE, ONT.

FORT HENRY, KINGSTON, ONT.

All these have been reconstructed, and are themselves object lessons in history. All contain exhibits of military uniforms, equipment, arms and artillery.

FORT WELLINGTON, PRESCOTT, ONT.

QUEEN'S UNIVERSITY, KINGSTON, ONT.

MURNEY TOWER, KINGSTON, ONT.

An historical monument containing military and pioneer relics.

MUSEUM, AMHERSTBURG, ONT.

Relics of Fort Malden and local material.

WILLISTEAD LIBRARY, WINDSOR, ONT.

George F. Macdonald collection of books, pictures and documents, many of them relating to the Detroit frontier.

UNIVERSITY OF WESTERN ONTARIO, LONDON, ONT.

The Lawson Memorial Library contains an extensive collection of items illustrating the local history of Western Ontario, in particular numbers of early agricultural journals, the J. Davis Barnett collection of books and clippings, many of them early technical and mechanical handbooks, and the thesis of C. J. Buck on Pioneer Arts and Architecture, profusely illustrated.

BRANT COUNTY HISTORICAL SOCIETY MUSEUM, PUBLIC LIBRARY, BRANTFORD, ONT.

Articles of domestic use, Indian relics, fire-fighting apparatus, lighting fixtures, and other pioneer relics.

NORFOLK HISTORICAL SOCIETY MUSEUM, SIMCOE, ONT.

Contains the collection of paintings of portraits and buildings by W. E. Cantelon.

PUBLIC LIBRARY, HAMILTON, ONT.

Contains many valuable books, documents and pictures relating to the history of the locality.

DUNDURN CASTLE, HAMILTON, ONT.

Itself a historical monument, it houses a collection of objects, furniture, utensils, weapons and pictures. Guide book, by Melville Bailey, gives full information regarding the buildings and exhibits.

WATERLOO HISTORICAL SOCIETY MUSEUM, PUBLIC LIBRARY, KITCHENER, ONT.

Files of early local newspapers, documents, relics and pictures, etc.

HURON INSTITUTE, COLLINGWOOD, ONT.

Large collection of pictures, etc., illustrating the history of shipping on the Great Lakes. Catalogue issued.

MUSEUM, NIAGARA-ON-THE-LAKE, ONT.

Extensive and valuable collection of local history material.

GAGE HOMESTEAD, STONEY CREEK, ONT.
Domestic furniture, portraits, scrap-books.

BRANT HOUSE, BURLINGTON, ONT.
Excellent reconstruction, with nucleus of museum, including some Brant relics.

THE PERKINS BULL COLLECTION, HIGH SCHOOL AND PUBLIC LIBRARY, BRAMPTON, ONT.
Extensive collection of pictures, relics, etc., relating to Peel County history.

PUBLIC ARCHIVES OF ONTARIO, TORONTO, ONT.
Many documents, newspaper files, pictures, etc.

J. ROSS ROBERTSON COLLECTION, PUBLIC LIBRARY, TORONTO, ONT.
Extensive collection of local views, portraits, etc., covering the history of Toronto and vicinity.

COLBORNE LODGE, HOWARD PARK, TORONTO, ONT.
Domestic articles, furniture, etc.

CANADIAN MILITARY INSTITUTE, TORONTO, ONT.
Uniforms, arms, books and documents.

ACADEMY OF MEDICINE, TORONTO, ONT.
Contains some interesting material illustrating early Ontario Medical history.

TEMPLE OF THE CHILDREN OF PEACE, SHARON, ONT.
Farm implements, household articles, etc.

BARNUM HOUSE, NEAR GRAFTON, ONT.
Fine example of early nineteenth century domestic architecture, restored, and furnished in style of period.

BYTOWN MUSEUM, OTTAWA, ONT.

MUSEUM OF HISTORICAL SOCIETY OF ARGENTEUIL COUNTY, CARILLON, QUE.

LAVAL UNIVERSITY, QUEBEC, QUE.

MUSÉE DE SÉMINAIRE DES TROIS RIVIÈRES, QUE.

MANOIR MAUVIDE-GENEST, ILE D'ORLEANS, QUE.
Excellent specimen of manor house, with collection of furniture, etc.

MANOIR RICHELIEU, MURRAY BAY, QUE.
Largest collection of early Canadian prints, paintings and drawings.

PUBLIC ARCHIVES OF NOVA SCOTIA, HALIFAX, N.S.
Portraits, views, ship models, etc.

PROVINCE HOUSE, HALIFAX, N.S.
Portraits, etc.

Public Library and Museum, Yarmouth, N.S.

Museum, Memorial Park, Grand Pré, N.S.

St. Edward's Church, Clementsport, N.S.

Museum, Green Hill, N.S.

De la Tour Museum, Centre East Pubnico, N.S.

Hudson's Bay Company Museum, Winnipeg, Man.

Large collection of objects connected with the history of Northern and Western Canada.

Cathedral, St. Boniface, Man.

Museum in crypt, containing Métis material, etc.

Saskatchewan Historical Society Museum, Regina, Sask.

University of Saskatchewan Museum, Saskatoon, Sask.

Museum, Battleford, Sask.

Provincial Museum, Victoria, B.C.

British Columbia Archives, Victoria, B.C

Researchers should consult the very full list of Canadian Historical Museum Collections, compiled by Miss G. M. Kidd, published in *The Canadian Historical Review*, September, 1940.